A Year of Holidays

Table of Contents

Dedication

For every cook who wants to celebrate special holidays all year long by making delicious meals for family & friends.

....

Appreciation

Thanks to everyone who shared their delightful and delicious recipes with us!

....

Gooseberry Patch
An imprint of Globe Pequot
246 Goose Lane • Guilford, CT 06437

www.gooseberrypatch.com
1•800•854•6673

Copyright © 2020, Gooseberry Patch
978-1-62093-401-2

Welcome

Dear Friends,

There is nothing more satisfying than preparing tasty meals for your family & friends any time of year. But as holidays come and go during the year, it is even more exciting to create memories with recipes that are sure to become family favorites.

A Year of Holidays *is the perfect cookbook to celebrate every special event in your year. Whether you are looking for a Halloween treat or a Christmas dinner...an Easter dessert or a 4th-of-July main dish, you'll find it in this book of tried & true recipes from* **Gooseberry Patch.**

Inside this book you'll find Halloween recipes like Jack-o'-Lantern Bread (page 18) and Scaredy-Cat Cookies (page 22). You'll love the Roast Turkey with Sage Butter (page 58) for that special Thanksgiving meal. Candy Cane Thumbprints (page 96) and Mrs. Claus' Christmas Bread (page 98) will make great homemade gifts for those special friends and neighbors. Potato Latkes (page 104) will be the perfect recipe to celebrate Hanukkah and Jo Ann's Holiday Brie (page 128) is an elegant appetizer for any holiday celebration. Need a simple Valentine treat? Try making some 2-Kiss Cupcakes (page 144) for that special someone. Spring and summer holidays mean outside fun and fresh ingredients. Try an Asparagus & Mushroom Omelet (page 174) or some Pecan-Stuffed Deviled Eggs (page 178). They will love it!

We are pleased to bring you this year-'round holiday cookbook that offers fresh, fun and satisfying recipes for every special day that you celebrate together. Enjoy!

Sincerely,
Jo Ann & Vickie

About this Book

We all enjoy every day of the week and every time of the year, but when a holiday comes near it is exciting and rewarding to showcase our cooking talents to share with family & friends. Holidays are a time to celebrate!

In this book you will find dozens of recipes to celebrate every special occasion throughout the year. We also give you ideas for presenting your holiday dishes in clever ways. Whether you are looking for some new recipes for a spooky Halloween party, a complete and festive menu for a Christmas gathering, some exciting ways to bring in the new year, a sweet goodie for your secret Valentine or a fresh new dinner idea for Easter, you will find just the recipes you need in this book of year-'round holiday recipes. You'll also find some tasty and traditional recipes for Hanukkah, some spicy dishes for Cinco de Mayo along with great treats for Mother's and Father's Day, 4th of July and more!

We know you will enjoy and treasure this fun-filled cookbook with clever recipes that you can make all year long...perfect recipes to make each celebration a happy holiday memory.

Introduction

Making the Holiday Special

Cooking for family & friends is so satisfying all year long, but during any holiday season it can become the focal point of the holiday. Many of our fondest memories revolve around the food that is served or presented during each holiday event. What do we remember about Thanksgiving? The Thanksgiving dinner! Can anyone think about Christmas without thinking about a tray of Christmas cookies? Valentine's Day brings back memories of sweet treats and Easter means lots of eggs in all kinds of recipes. In addition to the recipes that we serve and remember, the presentation of these yummy dishes is also important...and fun! Here are some tips for just a few of the holidays for making each celebration even more memorable.

Table Settings and Tablescapes

When your family & friends gather to celebrate each holiday, make the table the center of attention. Here are some ideas for some of the holidays you celebrate.

Halloween: Don't be afraid to be silly and spooky when you present your Halloween recipes. Add a plastic spider on the edge of the glass of a favorite drink and paint the name of each guest on mini pumpkins to serve as a place card.

Thanksgiving: Thanksgiving is all about giving thanks and enjoying the harvest. Choose a large wood tray or cutting board and arrange beautiful fruits and veggies on the tray and set it on a piece of fringed burlap to make a simple centerpiece.

Christmas: There are so many holiday themes to say "Merry Christmas" but oftentimes the season is so busy that a quick idea is the best. For a super-quick centerpiece, place a red candle in a low clear dish and surround it with fresh cranberries and little snips of evergreen. For a take-home table favor, fill clear ornaments with tiny jingle bells and add a ribbon through the hanger topper. Write each guest's name on the clear ornament with a permanent marker.

New Year's Day: Don't forget to celebrate the new year! Put a clock in the center of the table, set to 12:00, and surround it with confetti. Give each guest a party blower at their place.

Valentine's Day: Your favorite Valentine will love to see his or her name written on a paper tablecloth. Cover the table with a white or pink paper tablecloth and then draw hearts and names that spell out love. The kids can help with this table art. Set the table with clear plates so the guest can read the designs.

Mother's Day: This important day can be more memorable with a posie or two on the table. Place a tiny vase at each place setting and put one small bloom in the vase. Then tie a ribbon around the vase with the name of the guest.

Father's Day: Decorate a paper place mat with a list of all of the things that make Dad special. Then serve him his favorite meal!

Easter: Little plastic eggs are great for hiding eggs outside, but they also make quick table favors for each guest. Hide a little piece of candy in each one and decorate the outside of the egg with snippets of ribbon and sequins.

Entertaining Tips for Holiday Fun

Plan Ahead

Set the table a day ahead and then cover it with a clean tablecloth to keep the dishes and glasses from getting dusty. This will give you more time on the day of the party to add the final touches to the table.

Make It Sparkle

The day before, run the drinking glasses through the dishwasher before setting the table to make them sparkle. Hand-wash delicate items in advance as well.

Measure Up

The tablecloth should drop 11 to 18 inches from the edges of the table. Leave 12 inches between place settings if possible. The dinner plate (or charger) and flatware should sit one inch from the edge of the table.

Keep it Simple

Don't use highly scented flowers or candles on the table. They interfere with the aromas and flavors of the food...plus some guests may be sensitive to certain flowers or candles.

Look Across the Table

Centerpieces should be below eye level of seated guests so people can talk across the table easily.

Change it Up

Try serving dessert somewhere other than at the dining table, such as in the living room or on a four-season porch. This will allow guests to move around a bit before the final course.

The Proper Table Setting

Use this illustration to help you set the perfect holiday table.

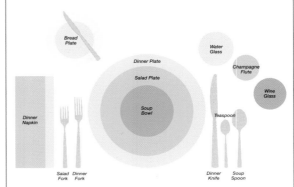

PLATES and BOWLS: Place the large plate directly on the table in the absence of a charger. Then set the salad plate atop the dinner plate. It should be removed after the salad course is eaten. If soup is being served, place the bowl on the salad plate. Place the small bread plate above and to the left of the dinner plate (directly above the forks).

FLATWARE: Set the large dinner fork to the immediate left of the dinner plate. Because the salad fork is used first, place it on the outside to the left of the dinner fork. The dinner knife goes to the immediate right of the dinner plate, with the blade facing inward. Place the teaspoon to the right of the dinner knife, with the bowl facing up. If soup is being served, the soup spoon should sit to the right of the teaspoon.

NAPKINS and GLASSES:
Place the dinner napkin to the left of the salad fork. For a more casual presentation (or if you're not using a soup bowl), place it on the salad plate. Place the water glass in easy reach above the dinner plate. Fill it with chilled water before guests are seated. Situate the champagne flute and/or wine glass to the right of the water glass. A red-wine glass is larger than a white-wine glass; its large bowl allows the wine to breathe.

Chapter One

Fall Celebrations

Celebrate autumn holidays and family get-togethers with recipes that are sure to please. Any little ghoul or boy would love to have a sweet Witches' Broom for a Halloween treat. The fall air might be crisp, but a bowl of Pumpkin Chowder will warm them up quickly. Looking for a quick comfort food for that Thanksgiving supper? Bake some delicious Cranberry Meatloaves and warm-and-toasty Squash Casserole...then finish the meal with the Perfect Pecan Pie. You'll delight them all with the tasty seasonal dishes you find in this chapter of fall favorites.

Lori Simmons, *Princeville, IL*

Cheesy Jack-o'-Lantern

This cheese ball looks just like a pumpkin... great for Halloween! If you have extra pepperoni, chop it finely and stir into the cream cheese mixture for a tasty addition.

Makes 3 cups

3 green onions, divided
2 8-oz. pkgs. cream cheese, softened
8-oz. pkg. shredded Cheddar cheese, divided
¼ c. red pepper, finely chopped
Garnish: several slices pepperoni
assorted crackers

Cut a 4-inch "stem" from the green part of one onion; chop remaining onions and set aside. In a bowl, beat together cream cheese and 1¼ cups Cheddar cheese. Stir in remaining onions and red pepper; cover and refrigerate one hour. Form into a ball; roll in remaining Cheddar cheese. Cut pepperoni slices into triangle shapes for eyes, nose and mouth; press into cheese ball to make a face. Insert reserved onion piece into top. Serve with assorted crackers.

> ⮞ **Fall Treats** ⮜
>
> After wrapping each apple in cellophane, nestle it inside a small orange gift sack. Add a pumpkin face to the sack using a black permanent marker, then gather the sack around the stick and tie on green curling ribbon.

Virginia Watson, *Scranton, PA*

Caramel Apples

Caramel apples are the stuff of fall festivals and Halloween carnivals! With each messy bite, they bring out the child in us all.

Makes 6 apples

6 Granny Smith apples
6 wooden craft sticks
14-oz. pkg. caramels, unwrapped
1 T. vanilla extract
1 T. water
2 c. chopped pecans or peanuts, toasted
Optional: 12-oz. bag semi-sweet chocolate
   chips, pecan halves

Wash and dry apples; remove stems. Insert a craft stick into stem end of each apple; set aside. Combine caramels, vanilla and water in a microwave-safe bowl. Microwave on high 90 seconds or until melted, stirring twice. Dip each apple into the caramel mixture quickly, allowing excess caramel to drip off. Roll in chopped nuts; place apples on lightly greased wax paper. Chill at least 15 minutes. If desired, to make chocolate-dipped caramel apples, microwave chocolate chips on high 90 seconds or until melted, stirring twice; cool 5 minutes. Pour chocolate where craft sticks and apples meet, allowing chocolate to drip down sides of caramel apples. Press pecan halves onto chocolate, if desired. Chill 15 minutes or until set.

Caramel Apples

Amy Thomason Hunt, *Traphill, NC*

Oktoberfest Pie

A wonderful easy meal to share after a day at the pumpkin patch. Add some pickled beets and hot rolls on the side...your family may just take you out for dessert!

Makes 6 servings

14-oz. pkg. Kielbasa turkey sausage, cut into
   ½-inch pieces
14-oz. can sauerkraut, drained
1 c. shredded Swiss cheese
¾ c. low-fat biscuit baking mix
½ c. skim milk
½ c. non-alcoholic beer
2 eggs, beaten

Spray a 9" glass pie plate with non-stick vegetable spray. Layer Kielbasa, sauerkraut and cheese in pie plate; set aside. In a bowl, stir together remaining ingredients until well blended; pour over cheese. Bake, uncovered, at 400 degrees for about 35 minutes. Let stand several minutes; cut into wedges.

Cindy Atkins, *Vancouver, WA*

Creamy Tuna Melts

Make your Halloween sandwiches full of fun by adding slices of black olives on top to make silly faces.

Serves 8

2 to 3 stalks celery, diced
1 onion, diced
12-oz. can tuna, drained
½ c. cottage cheese
½ c. mayonnaise
¼ t. garlic salt
⅛ t. sugar
4 English muffins, split and toasted
8 slices American cheese, cut into shapes
Optional: black olives

In a skillet sprayed with non-stick vegetable spray, sauté celery and onion until tender. Add tuna, cottage cheese, mayonnaise, garlic salt and sugar to skillet. Mix well, breaking up tuna. Cook over low heat until warmed through, stirring frequently; remove from heat. Place toasted muffins cut sides up on a broiler pan. Spread with tuna mixture; top with cheese pieces. If desired, top with black olives to form face. Broil until cheese melts; serve immediately.

Creamy Tuna Melts

Chocolatey Chewy Brownies

Jacklyn Akey, Merrill, WI

You'll love these chewy little squares of chocolate. Cut them into Halloween shapes for some extra fun!

Makes about 2 dozen

1 c. butter, softened
2 c. sugar
4 eggs, beaten
1 c. all-purpose flour
4 1-oz. sqs. unsweetened baking chocolate, melted
Optional: powdered sugar

In a bowl, beat butter and sugar with an electric mixer on medium speed, until creamy. Beat in eggs, mixing well. Stir in remaining ingredients. Pour into a greased and floured 13"x9" baking pan. Bake at 350 degrees for 30 minutes. Cool. Dust with powdered sugar, if desired. Cut into shapes or squares.

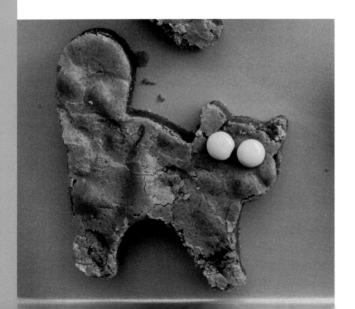

Witches' Brooms

Jennifer Peterson, Berwick, IA

Any witch would love to have a sweet broom like these yummy cookies!

Makes about 4 dozen

1 c. butter, softened
2 c. brown sugar, packed
2 eggs, beaten
4½ c. all-purpose flour
2 t. baking powder
1 t. baking soda
½ c. milk
1 t. vanilla extract
1 t. lemon extract
pretzel rods
Garnish: orange sugar

In a large bowl, combine all ingredients except pretzels and garnish; mix well. Cover; refrigerate for one hour. Roll out dough ½-inch thick on a floured surface. Cut out triangle shapes. Place on greased and floured baking sheet with pretzel rod tucked underneath. Add strip of dough at top of triangle. Use a fork to score bottom of triangle. Sprinkle with orange sugar. Bake at 350 degrees for 10 minutes, or until golden around edges. Cool for one minute before removing from baking sheets; cool completely on wax paper.

Witches' Brooms

Joyce Stackhouse, *Cadiz, OH*

Pumpkin Pudding

This recipe is really quick to make and scrumptious...perfect for a light dessert after a big meal. If you are watching your calories, you can use sugar-free pudding mix and skim milk.

Makes 6 to 8 servings

2 c. milk
3.4-oz. pkg. instant vanilla pudding mix
1 c. canned pumpkin
1 t. vanilla extract
1 t. pumpkin pie spice
½ t. cinnamon
Optional: whipped cream

Combine milk and dry pudding mix in a large bowl. Beat with an electric mixer on low speed for one to 2 minutes, until smooth. Add pumpkin, vanilla and spices; mix well. Spoon into individual dessert bowls; cover and chill. If desired, garnish with dollops of whipped cream at serving time.

Jo Ann, *Gooseberry Patch*

Jack-o'-Lantern Bread

Kids love these! Marinara sauce is great for dipping.

Serves 10 to 12

2 1-lb. loaves frozen bread dough, thawed
1 T. egg, beaten
1½ t. milk

Place the loaves in a bowl. Cover bowl with plastic wrap and let rise until doubled, 45 minutes to one hour. Punch dough down, knead loaves together in bowl and shape into a ball. Transfer ball to a greased 15"x12" baking sheet. With greased hands or a lightly floured rolling pin, flatten ball into a 13"x11" oval. Cut out eyes, nose and mouth; openings should be at least 1½ to 2 inches wide. (To make small loaves, divide dough into 4 equal pieces and roll into 6"x4" ovals; eye, nose and mouth openings should be at least one to 1½ inches wide.) Lift out cut-out dough and bake on another pan or use for decoration. Cover the shaped dough lightly with plastic wrap and let rise until puffy, about 20 minutes. Mix egg with milk; brush over dough. Bake at 350 degrees for 30 to 35 minutes or until golden. Cool on a wire rack. Serve warm or cool.

Jack-o'-Lantern Bread

Jennie Gist, *Gooseberry Patch*

Swampwater Dressing

Serve this zingy dressing alongside a leafy green salad at your Halloween "Boo"-ffet!

Makes about 1½ cups

1 c. oil
6 T. cider vinegar
½ c. sugar
1 t. celery seed
½ t. salt
¼ t. pepper

Combine ingredients in a jar or plastic container with a tight-fitting lid; cover. Shake well until dressing is blended and sugar dissolves. Keep refrigerated.

Lizzy Burnley, *Ankeny, IA*

Spooky Salad

This tasty recipe uses a bit of pasta to make a spooky-looking bowl of healthy goodness.

Makes 4 servings

6 c. butter leaf lettuce or green leaf lettuce, torn
1 c. canned mandarin oranges, drained
⅓ c. sliced ripe olives
¼ c. sunflower seed kernals
1 c. cooked spaghetti

In a large salad bowl, toss together all ingredients. Drizzle Swampwater Dressing or other favorite dressing over salad, tossing gently to coat. Serve immediately.

> ∼ **Just for Fun** ∼
>
> It's the unexpected touches that make the biggest impression when you are having a party. Don't be afraid to be a little silly at your Halloween bash...a plastic spider on the dressing pitcher will bring a smile.

Spooky Salad

Dale Duncan, *Waterloo, IA*

Silver Moons

Your little werewolves will be howling for more!

Makes 8

1 T. sugar
¼ t. cinnamon
16.3-oz. tube refrigerated large biscuits
1 c. apple pie filling
4 t. butter, melted
Garnish: powdered sugar

In a small bowl, combine sugar and cinnamon; set aside. Separate dough into 8 biscuits. Press each biscuit into a 5-inch circle. Arrange biscuits on greased baking sheets. Place 2 tablespoons pie filling on each circle half. Fold biscuits over filling; seal edges with a fork. Pierce each pie a few times with fork. Brush pies with melted butter and sprinkle with sugar mixture. Bake at 375 degrees for 15 to 20 minutes. Sprinkle with powdered sugar. Serve warm.

Kay Marone, *Des Moines, IA*

Scaredy-Cat Cookies

Kids love to make and eat these cute Halloween goodies!

Makes 2 dozen

1 c. butter, softened
2 c. sugar
2 eggs, beaten
1 T. vanilla extract
3 c. all-purpose flour
1 c. baking cocoa
½ t. baking powder
½ t. baking soda
½ t. salt
48 pieces candy corn
24 red cinnamon candies

In a bowl, combine butter and sugar. Beat in eggs and vanilla. In a separate bowl, combine flour, cocoa, baking powder, baking soda and salt; gradually add to butter mixture. Roll dough into 1½ inch balls. Place 3 inches apart on lightly greased baking sheets. Flatten with a glass dipped in sugar. Pinch tops of cookies to form ears. For whiskers, press a fork twice into each cookie. Bake at 350 degrees for 7 to 8 minutes, until almost set. Remove from oven; immediately press on candy corn for eyes and cinnamon candies for noses. Remove to wire racks to cool.

Scaredy-Cat Cookies

Sherry Sheehan, *Phoenix, AZ*

Eyeball Soup in a Slow Cooker

Don't be scared away by this tasty soup's name...the eyeballs are actually meatballs!

Serves 8

2 lbs. lean ground beef
1 c. Italian-seasoned dry bread crumbs
1 egg, beaten
Optional: ¼ c. olive oil
3 stalks celery, sliced
1 green pepper, diced
1 c. carrots, peeled and diced
15¼-oz. can corn, drained
2 14-oz. cans beef broth
10-oz. can diced tomatoes with green chiles
4-oz. can diced green chiles
3 c. cooked rice
2 T. fresh cilantro, finely chopped
2 T. onion, minced
1 t. garlic powder
1 t. ground cumin
1 t. chili powder
1 t. salt
½ t. pepper
4 to 5 c. water

Combine ground beef, bread crumbs and egg; form into one-inch balls. Brown in a skillet over medium heat, adding oil, if desired; drain. Place meatballs in a 5-quart slow cooker and set aside. In a small saucepan, cover celery, green pepper and carrots with a little water. Cook until tender; add to slow cooker with remaining ingredients. Cover and cook on low setting 3 to 4 hours.

Sandy Westendorp, *Grand Rapids, MI*

Pumpkin Chowder

This blend of everyday ingredients is anything but ordinary.

Serves 6

½ lb. bacon, diced
2 c. onion, chopped
2 t. curry powder
2 T. all-purpose flour
1-lb. pie pumpkin, peeled, seeded and chopped
2 potatoes, peeled and cubed
4 c. chicken broth
1 c. half-and-half
salt and pepper to taste
Garnish: toasted pumpkin seeds, sliced green onions

Brown bacon in a stockpot over medium heat for 5 minutes; add onion. Sauté for 10 minutes; add curry powder and flour, stirring until smooth and creamy, about 5 minutes. Add pumpkin, potatoes and broth; simmer until pumpkin and potatoes are tender, about 15 minutes. Pour in half-and-half; season with salt and pepper. Simmer for 5 minutes; do not boil. Spoon into soup bowls; garnish with pumpkin seeds and green onions.

Pumpkin Chowder

Vickie, *Gooseberry Patch*

Cemetery Cookie Dessert

Little cookies stand up to resemble little tombstones on this easy-to-make dessert.

Serves 10 to 12

18-oz. pkg. chocolate sandwich cookies, divided
8-oz. pkg. cream cheese, softened
3.4-oz. pkg. instant vanilla pudding mix
2 c. milk
1 c. powdered sugar
8-oz. container frozen whipped topping, thawed
Garnish: candy pumpkins

Set aside 6 to 7 cookies for garnish; crush remaining cookies. Spread ¼ of crushed cookies in the bottom of a lightly greased 13"x9" glass baking pan; set aside. In a large bowl, whip cream cheese with an electric mixer on medium speed. In a separate bowl, whisk together dry pudding mix and milk for 2 minutes, or until thickened; add to cream cheese along with powdered sugar and whipped topping. Beat until well blended. Spoon a layer of cream cheese mixture over cookies; add another layer of crushed cookies and another layer of cream cheese mixture. Repeat once more, for a total of 3 layers. Slice sides off reserved cookies and arrange on top. Add candy pumpkins. Cover and chill for 2 hours before serving. Keep refrigerated.

Elijah Dahlstrom, *Ames, IA*

Wormy Popcorn Balls

Add a gummy worm to this little treat for some Halloween fun.

Makes about 10

20 c. popped popcorn
2 c. sugar
½ c. water
⅔ c. corn syrup
1 t. vanilla extract
1 t. salt
1 c. gummy worm candies

Place popcorn in a large heat-proof bowl; set aside. In a saucepan over medium heat, mix together remaining ingredients except worm candies. Bring to a boil. Stir mixture until it reaches the thread stage, or 230 to 233 degrees on a candy thermometer. Pour over popcorn; mix well and form into balls with well-buttered hands. Poke a hole with finger and add gummy worms. Reform ball as needed. Wrap balls in squares of wax paper.

Wormy Popcorn Balls

Kendall Hale, *Lynn, MA*

Pumpkin Spice Bars

Watch these bars disappear fast!

Makes 2 dozen

18¼-oz. pkg. spice cake mix
½ c. plus 1 T. butter, melted and divided
½ c. pecans, finely chopped
1 T. plus 1 t. vanilla extract, divided
8-oz. pkg. cream cheese, softened
⅓ c. light brown sugar, packed
1 c. canned pumpkin
1 egg
½ c. white chocolate, finely chopped
⅓ c. long-cooking oats, uncooked
Optional: powdered sugar

Combine cake mix, ½ cup melted butter, pecans and one tablespoon vanilla, mixing well with a fork. Reserve one cup crumbs for streusel topping. Press remaining crumbs into a lightly greased 13"x9" baking pan. Bake at 350 degrees for 13 to 15 minutes or until puffy and set. Cool in pan on a wire rack 20 minutes. Beat cream cheese at medium speed with an electric mixer 30 seconds or until creamy. Add brown sugar, pumpkin, egg and remaining vanilla; beat until blended. Pour filling over baked crust. Stir white chocolate, remaining melted butter and oats into reserved streusel. Sprinkle over filling. Bake at 350 degrees for 30 minutes or until edges begin to brown and center is set. Cool completely in pan on a wire rack. Sprinkle with powdered sugar, if desired. Cut into bars. Serve at room temperature or chilled.

Carrie Kelderman, *Pella, IA*

Jack-o'-Lantern Jumble

This is a sweet & savory mix that our kids request each fall. Whenever we share it with our extended family, it's gone in a flash!

Makes 10 cups

8 c. bite-size crispy corn & rice cereal squares
1 c. dry-roasted peanuts
¼ c. butter, sliced
¼ c. creamy peanut butter
2¼ t. Worcestershire sauce
¼ t. garlic salt
1 to 2 c. candy corn

Combine cereal and peanuts in a large bowl; set aside. In a saucepan, combine remaining ingredients except candy corn. Cook over low heat until melted, stirring frequently. Pour over cereal mixture, stirring to coat well. Spread in a lightly greased 15"x10" jelly-roll pan. Bake, uncovered, at 250 degrees for one hour. Cool to room temperature; stir in candy corn. Store in an airtight container.

Jack-o'-Lantern Jumble

Marian Buckley, *Fontana, CA*

Chow-Down Corn Chowder

So easy to prepare with a slow cooker. It's delicious! Perfect for a fall meal.

Serves 4

6 slices bacon, diced
½ c. onion, chopped
2 c. potatoes, peeled and diced
2 10-oz. pkgs. frozen corn
16-oz. can cream-style corn
1¼ T. sugar
1½ t. Worcestershire sauce
1¼ t. seasoned salt
½ t. pepper
1 c. water

In a skillet, fry bacon until crisp. Remove bacon; reserve drippings. Add onion and potatoes to drippings and sauté about 5 minutes; drain well. Combine all ingredients in a 3½-quart slow cooker; stir well. Cover and cook on low setting 4 to 7 hours.

⌐ Perfect Pairings ⌐

Nothing goes better with hearty chili than warm cornbread! If you like your cornbread crisp, prepare it in a vintage sectioned cast-iron skillet...each wedge of cornbread will bake up with its own golden crust.

Linda Marshall, *Ontario, Canada*

Black Beans & Vegetable Chili

This vegetarian chili filled with black beans, bell peppers, squash and tomatoes and served over rice is hearty and filling.

Makes 6 cups

1 onion, coarsely chopped
1 T. oil
28-oz. can diced tomatoes
⅔ c. picante sauce
1½ t. ground cumin
1 t. salt
½ t. dried basil
15-oz. can black beans, rinsed and drained
1 green pepper, cut into ¾-inch pieces
1 red pepper, cut into ¾-inch pieces
1 yellow squash or zucchini, cut into
   ½-inch pieces
hot cooked rice
Garnish: shredded Cheddar cheese, sour
   cream, chopped fresh cilantro
Optional: additional picante sauce

Sauté onion in oil in a Dutch oven over medium-high heat, stirring constantly, until tender. Add tomatoes with juice and next 4 ingredients; stir well. Bring to a boil; cover, reduce heat and simmer 5 minutes. Stir in beans, peppers and squash. Cover and cook over medium-low heat 25 minutes or until vegetables are tender, stirring mixture occasionally. To serve, ladle chili over rice in individual bowls. Top each serving with cheese, sour cream and cilantro. Serve with additional picante sauce, if desired.

Black Beans & Vegetable Chili

Ellen Folkman, *Crystal Beach, FL*

Spicy Citrus Cider

Keep this flavorful beverage warm in a slow cooker...everyone can help themselves.

Makes about 3 quarts

8 c. apple juice
2¼ c. water
1½ c. orange juice
¼ c. molasses
3 4-inch cinnamon sticks
1 T. whole cloves
Garnish: apple and orange slices

Combine all ingredients except fruit slices in a large saucepan over medium heat. Simmer for 10 minutes, stirring occasionally. Strain before serving. Garnish with fruit slices.

Jo Ann, *Gooseberry Patch*

Pumpkin Patch Cheese Ball

Makes a tasty cheese ball any time of year... but especially fun at Halloween!

Makes 10 to 12 servings

16-oz. pkg. shredded extra-sharp Cheddar
    cheese
8-oz. pkg. cream cheese, softened
8-oz. container chive & onion cream cheese
2 t. paprika
½ t. cayenne pepper
Garnish: honey-wheat twist pretzel, flat-leaf
    parsley leaves
assorted crackers

In a medium bowl, combine cheeses and spices. Cover and refrigerate for 4 hours. Shape mixture into a ball; lightly press into a pumpkin shape. Smooth surface with a table knife. Press pretzel and parsley into top of cheese ball for pumpkin stem and leaf. Serve with crackers.

Pumpkin Patch Cheese Ball

Barb Rudyk, *Alberta, Canada*

Baked Apple Pancake

Mmm...tender apples, brown sugar and cinnamon all combine to make these yummy baked pancakes.

Serves 6 to 8

4 apples, peeled, cored and sliced
1/2 c. butter, softened and divided
1/2 c. brown sugar, packed
1 t. cinnamon
6 eggs, beaten
1 c. all-purpose flour
1 c. milk
3 T. sugar

Combine apples, 1/4 cup butter, brown sugar and cinnamon in a microwave-safe bowl. Microwave on high setting about 2 to 4 minutes, until tender. Stir; spoon into a lightly greased 13"x9" baking pan and set aside. In a separate bowl, combine remaining ingredients; whisk until smooth and spread over apple mixture. Bake, uncovered, at 425 degrees for 25 minutes. Cut into squares; serve warm.

Athena Colegrove, *Big Springs, TX*

Spiderweb Cookies

Tuck these in cellophane bags, tie with twine and attach a spider ring...creepy and cute!

Makes 16

16 1/2-oz. tube refrigerated sugar cookie dough
3 c. powdered sugar
3 T. light corn syrup
1/2 t. vanilla extract
3 T. plus 3 t. milk, divided
2 T. baking cocoa

Slice dough into 16 rounds. Place 2 inches apart on ungreased baking sheets. Bake at 350 degrees for 12 to 14 minutes. Transfer to a wire rack to cool. Blend powdered sugar, corn syrup, vanilla and 3 tablespoons plus one teaspoon milk until smooth. Measure 1/3 cup of frosting mixture into a small bowl; stir in cocoa and remaining milk. Transfer chocolate frosting to a plastic zipping bag; snip off corner. Turn cookies so flat sides are up. Working on one cookie at a time, spread white frosting over top. Beginning in the center, pipe on a spiral of chocolate frosting. Starting in center of spiral, pull a knife tip through the spiral to create spiderweb pattern.

Spiderweb Cookies

Betty Kidd, *Washington, DC*

Monster Meatball Sandwiches

Make plenty of these sandwiches...they'll love them!

Makes 16

32 frozen bite-size meatballs
9-oz. jar mango chutney
1 c. chicken broth
16 dinner rolls
16-oz. jar sweet-hot pickle sandwich relish

Stir together first 3 ingredients in a medium saucepan. Bring to a boil over medium-high heat. Reduce heat to low and simmer, stirring occasionally, 25 to 30 minutes. Cut rolls vertically through top, cutting to, but not through bottom. Place 2 meatballs in each roll. Top with relish.

Sandy Ward, *Anderson, IN*

Harvest Moon Punch

Float little stars cut from apples as a garnish to this simple-to-stir-up drink.

Makes about one gallon

2 qts. apple cider
1 c. lemon juice
½ c. sugar
2 ltrs. ginger ale, chilled

In a punch bowl or large pitcher, combine cider, lemon juice and sugar. Stir until sugar dissolves. Cover and chill. Add ginger ale just before serving.

Jessica Kraus, *Delaware, OH*

Halloween Sloppy Joes

A staple at my house for Halloween night. Everyone loves it!

Makes 6 servings

1 lb. ground beef
1 onion, chopped
1 c. catsup
¼ c. water
2 T. brown sugar, packed
1 T. cider vinegar
1 t. Worcestershire sauce
6 hamburger buns, split

Brown beef and onion in a skillet over medium heat; drain. Stir in remaining ingredients except buns; reduce heat to medium-low. Simmer for 25 minutes, stirring occasionally. To serve, spoon onto buns.

Harvest Moon Punch

Anna Burns, *Delaware, OH*

Puffy Marshmallow Cut-Outs

The kids always love these!

Makes about 2 dozen

¾ c. water
4 envs. unflavored gelatin
3 c. sugar
1¼ c. light corn syrup
¼ t. salt
2 t. vanilla extract
1½ c. powdered sugar, divided

Spray a 13"x9" baking pan with non-stick vegetable spray. Line bottom and sides of pan with wax paper, allowing 2 to 4 inches to extend over edges of pan; coat wax paper with non-stick vegetable spray and set aside. Pour water into a large bowl and sprinkle gelatin over top; let stand 5 minutes. In a heavy saucepan, combine sugar, corn syrup, salt and vanilla; bring to a boil over high heat and cook until mixture reaches the soft-ball stage, or 234 to 243 degrees on a candy thermometer, stirring occasionally. Pour the hot mixture slowly into the gelatin mixture and beat by hand or with an electric mixer at medium speed for 10 minutes, or until very stiff. Pour into prepared pan; smooth top with a spatula. Let stand, uncovered, overnight or until mixture becomes firm. Invert the baking pan onto a surface coated with one cup powdered sugar; peel off wax paper. Lightly coat the insides of desired cookie cutters with non-stick vegetable spray and cut out marshmallows. Place remaining powdered sugar in a shallow dish; roll marshmallow cut-outs in powdered sugar to coat.

Vickie, *Gooseberry Patch*

Caramel-Pecan Popcorn Crunch

These crisp, buttery popcorn clusters with toasted pecans rival any sweet popcorn snack you can buy at the store.

Makes 25 cups

2 c. pecan halves
2 3½-oz. pkgs. natural-flavored microwave
    popcorn, popped
2 c. light brown sugar, packed
½ c. butter
½ c. light corn syrup
2 t. vanilla extract
½ t. almond extract
½ t. salt
½ t. baking soda

Bake pecans in a single layer in a shallow pan at 350 degrees for 8 to 10 minutes or until lightly toasted and fragrant. Reduce oven temperature to 250 degrees. Combine popcorn and pecans in a lightly greased 16"x12"x3" roasting pan. Combine brown sugar, butter and corn syrup in a 2½-quart heavy saucepan. Bring to a boil over medium-high heat, stirring until butter melts. Wash down sides of pan with a brush dipped in hot water. Cook mixture until it reaches the hard-ball stage, or 250 to 269 degrees on a candy thermometer, about 4 minutes. (Do not stir.) Remove from heat; stir in extracts, salt and baking soda. Gradually pour brown sugar mixture over popcorn and nuts, stirring gently to coat well, using a long-handled spoon. Bake at 250 degrees for 1½ hours or until dry, stirring occasionally. Cool completely in pan. Break into clusters and store in an airtight container up to 2 weeks.

Caramel-Pecan Popcorn Crunch

Lynda Robson, *Boston, MA*

Slow-Cooker Sloppy Joes

This is a perfect sandwich to serve after raking leaves.

Serves 14 to 18

3 c. celery, chopped
1 c. onion, chopped
1 c. catsup
1 c. barbecue sauce
1 c. water
2 T. vinegar
2 T. Worcestershire sauce
2 T. brown sugar, packed
1 t. chili powder
1 t. salt
1 t. pepper
½ t. garlic powder
3 to 4-lb. boneless chuck roast
14 to 18 hamburger buns
Optional: banana peppers, sliced olives, carrot crinkles, pretzel sticks, sliced pimentos, fresh parsley sprigs

Combine the first 12 ingredients in a 4 to 5-quart slow cooker; mix well. Add roast; cover and cook on high setting 6 to 7 hours or until tender. Remove roast; shred meat, return to slow cooker and heat through. Serve on hamburger buns. Garnish as desired.

> ── **Keep it Hot** ──
>
> If you're taking a casserole to a potluck dinner or picnic, keep it toasty by covering the casserole dish with aluminum foil and then wrapping it in several layers of newspaper.

Vickie, *Gooseberry Patch*

Squash Casserole

There's something about a classic vegetable casserole that's impossible to resist. Even picky eaters go back for second helpings!

Serves 8

1½ lbs. yellow squash, cut into ¼-inch slices
1 lb. zucchini, cut into ¼-inch slices
1 sweet onion, chopped
2½ t. salt, divided
1 c. carrots, peeled grated
10¾-oz. can cream of chicken soup
8-oz. container sour cream
8-oz. can water chestnuts, drained and chopped
8-oz. pkg. herb-flavored stuffing mix
½ c. butter, melted

Place squash and zucchini in a Dutch oven. Add chopped onion, 2 teaspoons salt and enough water to cover. Bring to a boil over medium-high heat and cook 5 minutes; drain well. Stir together carrot, next 3 ingredients and remaining salt in a large bowl; fold in squash mixture. Stir together stuffing mix and melted butter; spoon half of stuffing mixture into bottom of a lightly greased 13"x9" baking pan. Spoon squash mixture over stuffing mixture and top with remaining stuffing mixture. Bake at 350 degrees for 30 to 35 minutes or until bubbly and golden, covering with aluminum foil after 20 to 25 minutes to prevent excessive browning, if necessary. Let stand 10 minutes before serving.

Squash Casserole

Emma Brown, *Saskatchewan, Canada*

Maple Pork Chops

The sweetness of the maple syrup and saltiness of the soy sauce go so well together. My family can't get enough of these...I usually have to double the recipe!

Makes 4 servings

½ c. maple syrup
3 T. soy sauce
2 cloves garlic, minced
4 pork chops

In a bowl, whisk together syrup, soy sauce and garlic; reserve ¼ cup of mixture. Add pork chops to remaining mixture in bowl. Cover and refrigerate for at least 15 minutes to overnight. Drain, discarding mixture in bowl. Grill over medium-high heat until browned and cooked through, about 6 minutes per side. Drizzle pork chops with reserved syrup mixture before serving.

Jo Ann, *Gooseberry Patch*

Caramelized Vidalia Onion Dip

Here's a new take on an old favorite appetizer. Look for sturdy sweet potato chips for scooping up this mega-cheesy family favorite.

Makes 4 cups

2 T. butter
3 Vidalia or other sweet onions, thinly sliced
8-oz. pkg. cream cheese, softened
8-oz. pkg. Swiss cheese, shredded
1 c. grated Parmesan cheese
1 c. mayonnaise
sweet potato chips

Melt butter in a large skillet over medium heat; add sliced onions. Cook, stirring often, 30 to 40 minutes or until onions are caramel colored. Combine onions, cheeses and mayonnaise, stirring well. Spoon dip into a lightly greased 1½ to 2-quart casserole dish. Bake, uncovered, at 375 degrees for 30 minutes or until golden and bubbly. Serve with sweet potato chips.

⟿ So Simple ⟾

Make your own tortilla chips to go with salsas and dips...you won't believe how easy it is. Just slice flour tortillas into wedges, spray with non-stick vegetable spray and bake at 350 degrees for 5 to 7 minutes.

Caramelized Vidalia Onion Dip

Connie Herek, *Bay City, MI*

Mini Pumpkin Spice Loaves

This is a perfect bread to make and give away as little unexpected gifts to family and friends. Just slide the cooled bread into plastic zipping bags and tie a ribbon around the bags.

Makes 12 mini loaves

¾ c. butter, softened
3 c. sugar
3 eggs
3 c. all-purpose flour
2 t. baking powder
1 t. baking soda
½ t. salt
1 t. cinnamon
1 t. ground cloves
¼ t. nutmeg
1 c. chopped pecans, toasted
¾ c. golden raisins
2 c. canned pumpkin
1 t. vanilla extract

Beat butter at medium speed with an electric mixer until creamy. Gradually add sugar, beating well. Add eggs, one at a time, beating just until yellow disappears after each addition. Combine flour and next 6 ingredients in a medium bowl. Add pecans and raisins, tossing to coat. Add flour mixture to butter mixture alternately with pumpkin, beginning and ending with flour mixture. Stir in vanilla. Spoon batter into 12 greased and floured 5"x3" mini loaf pans. Bake at 325 degrees for 45 minutes or until a toothpick inserted in center comes out clean. Cool in pans on a wire rack 10 minutes; remove from pans and let cool completely. Frost loaves with Cream Cheese Icing.

CREAM CHEESE ICING:

3-oz. pkg. cream cheese, softened
3 T. butter, softened
½ t. vanilla extract
2¾ c. powdered sugar
2 T. milk

Beat first 3 ingredients at medium speed with an electric mixer until creamy; gradually add powdered sugar, beating until smooth. Add milk, one tablespoon at a time, beating until spreading consistency. (Icing will be thick.) Makes 1¾ cup.

> ~ **Perfect Pairings** ~
> This bread is sweet, but it goes so well with a breakfast or lunch omelet and some crisp bacon. A perfect fall meal!

Mini Pumpkin Spice Loaves

Mary Murray, *Mount Vernon, OH*

October Bisque

Even though I call this "October Bisque" it is good any month of the year.

Makes 8 servings

1 onion, chopped
¼ c. butter
4 c. chicken broth
28-oz. can whole tomatoes
1 T. sugar
2 15-oz. cans pumpkin
2 T. fresh parsley, chopped
2 T. fresh chives, chopped

Sauté onion in butter until onion is tender. Add broth and simmer for 15 minutes. Place tomatoes in a blender or food processor and blend until smooth. Add tomato mixture, sugar, pumpkin, parsley and chives to broth; heat through.

~ **Cooking Tip** ~

In the fall, be sure your pantry is stocked with plenty of canned pumpkin. It can be used in so many ways...pies, breads, soups and more.

Lisanne Miller, *Wells, ME*

3-Cheese Pasta Bake

This yummy mac & cheese dish gets a great update with penne pasta and a trio of cheeses.

Serves 4

8-oz. pkg. pasta, uncooked
2 T. butter
2 T. all-purpose flour
1½ c. milk
½ c. half-and-half
1 c. shredded white Cheddar cheese
¼ c. grated Parmesan cheese
2 c. shredded Gruyère cheese, divided
1 t. salt
¼ t. pepper
⅛ t. nutmeg

Prepare pasta according to package directions. Meanwhile, melt butter in a saucepan over medium heat. Whisk in flour until smooth; cook, whisking constantly, one minute. Gradually whisk in milk and half-and-half; cook, whisking constantly, 3 to 5 minutes or until thickened. Stir in Cheddar cheese, Parmesan cheese, one cup Gruyère cheese and next 3 ingredients until smooth. Stir together pasta and cheese mixture; pour into a lightly greased 11"x7" baking pan. Top with remaining Gruyère cheese. Bake, uncovered, at 350 degrees for 15 minutes or until golden and bubbly.

3-Cheese Pasta Bake

Kristin Stone, *Davis, CA*

Ghostly Pizza

Everyone loves pizza! Use fresh mozzarella cheese and watch it melt into little ghosts.

Serves 6

3 c. bread flour
1 t. salt
½ t. sugar
1 c. warm water, 110 to 115 degrees
1 T. oil
1 T. quick-rising yeast
Garnish: favorite pizza toppings

In a bowl, combine flour, salt and sugar. Add water, oil and yeast to bowl. Knead by hand for 3 minutes; form into a ball. Cover and let rise until double in bulk, about an hour. Punch down dough; let rest for 4 minutes. Divide dough into 2 balls. On a floured surface, roll out each ball about ¼-inch thick. Place on ungreased baking sheets. Let rise an additional 10 to 15 minutes. Spread Pizza Sauce over dough; add desired toppings. Place pizza in a cold oven; turn to 500 degrees. Bake for 17 to 20 minutes, until golden.

PIZZA SAUCE:

8-oz. can tomato sauce
6-oz. can tomato paste
1¼ t. dried oregano
1¼ t. dried basil
1¼ t. garlic powder
1 t. salt

Stir together ingredients in a medium bowl.

Becky Drees, *Pittsfield, MA*

Trail Mix Bagels

Perfect for an on-the-go dinner, lunch or autumn hike...a tasty energy boost!

Makes 4 servings

8-oz. pkg. cream cheese, softened
1 T. lemon juice
½ c. raisins
1 carrot, peeled and grated
⅓ c. trail mix, coarsely chopped, or sunflower kernels
4 bagels, split

Place cream cheese in a bowl. Add remaining ingredients except bagels; stir until well blended and creamy. Spread between sliced bagels.

Trail Mix Bagels

Jo Ann, *Gooseberry Patch*

Pork Chops, Cabbage & Apples

Pork, cabbage and apples make a classic combination that's just delightful!

Serves 6

3 t. paprika, divided
2 t. chopped fresh or 1 t. dried thyme, divided
2 t. kosher salt, divided
1½ t. pepper, divided
2 t. chopped fresh or 1 t. dried sage, divided
6 ½-inch-thick bone-in pork loin chops
2 slices bacon
1 head cabbage, coarsely chopped
2 onions, thinly sliced
1 Granny Smith apple, peeled and sliced
1 T. tomato paste
12-oz. bottle lager beer or 1½ c. apple cider
Optional: fresh thyme sprigs

Combine 2 teaspoons paprika, one teaspoon fresh or ½ teaspoon dried thyme, one teaspoon salt, one teaspoon pepper and one teaspoon fresh or ½ teaspoon dried sage; rub over pork chops. Cook bacon slices in a large, deep skillet over medium-high heat 6 to 8 minutes or until crisp. Remove bacon and drain on paper towels, reserving drippings in skillet. Crumble bacon. Cook pork in hot drippings 3 minutes on each side or until browned and done; remove pork from skillet and keep warm. Add cabbage, onions and apple to skillet. Cover and reduce heat to medium; cook, stirring occasionally, 15 minutes or until cabbage begins to wilt. Add tomato paste, beer or apple cider, bacon, remaining paprika, thyme, salt, pepper and sage, stirring to loosen particles from bottom of skillet. Cover and cook 15 minutes or until cabbage is tender and liquid is slightly thickened. Add pork and cook, uncovered, 5 minutes or until thoroughly heated. Garnish with fresh thyme sprigs, if desired.

Sheryl Eastman, *Wixom, MI*

Sausage & Apple Kraut

Serve with mashed potatoes, buttered green beans and fresh-baked rolls for a satisfying chilly-weather meal.

Makes 4 to 6 servings

27-oz. jar sauerkraut, drained, rinsed and divided
1 lb. Kielbasa sausage, sliced and divided
2 tart apples, peeled, cored and diced
½ c. brown sugar, packed and divided
2 c. apple cider or juice, divided

In a lightly greased 13"x9" baking pan, layer half of sauerkraut, half of sausage and all the apples. Sprinkle with ¼ cup brown sugar. Pour one cup cider or juice over top. Repeat layering. Cover and bake at 350 degrees for 1½ hours, or until sauerkraut is caramelized and golden.

Sausage & Apple Kraut

Leigh Ellen Eades, *Summersville, WV*

Black Cherry & Cranberry Salad

I remember my mother making this salad for Thanksgiving and Christmas when I was a child. Now, it's at the top of my own holiday menus!

Makes 8 servings

8-oz. can crushed pineapple
¼ c. water
3-oz. pkg. black cherry gelatin mix
16-oz. can whole-berry cranberry sauce
1 c. celery, chopped
1 c. chopped walnuts
¼ c. lemon juice

In a saucepan over medium heat, mix undrained pineapple and water. Heat to boiling; add gelatin mix and stir until gelatin is dissolved. Add remaining ingredients and stir well. Transfer to a 6-cup serving dish. Chill in refrigerator for 4 hours, or until firm.

Sue Steadman, *Phoenix, AZ*

Turkey Panini

Use leftover turkey after a big holiday feast for these delicious sandwiches. Pile on the turkey and use your homemade cranberry sauce, if desired. Shaved deli turkey is a fine substitute.

Makes 2 sandwiches

¼ c. whole-berry cranberry sauce
2 to 3 t. horseradish
2 T. mayonnaise
4 ½-inch-thick large slices ciabatta bread
4 ⅜-inch-thick slices cooked turkey breast or deli turkey
salt and pepper to taste
4 slices provolone cheese
4 slices bacon, cooked
1½ T. olive oil
Optional: mixed salad greens

Preheat the panini press according to manufacturer's instructions. Combine cranberry sauce and horseradish, stirring well. Spread mayonnaise on one side of each slice of bread. Spread cranberry-horseradish sauce on 2 slices of bread; top each sandwich with 2 turkey slices and sprinkle with salt and pepper. Arrange 2 cheese slices on each sandwich; top with 2 bacon slices. Cover with tops of bread, mayonnaise side down. Brush tops of sandwiches with olive oil. Turn and brush bottoms of sandwiches with olive oil. Place sandwiches in panini press; cook 3 minutes or until cheese begins to melt and bread is toasted. Serve hot. Garnish with mixed salad greens, if desired.

Turkey Panini

Nancy Wise, *Little Rock, AR*

Ultimate Nachos

We love to serve this when we tailgate at our favorite football games.

Serves 6 to 8

1/3 c. onion, finely chopped
1 clove garlic, minced
1 T. olive oil
16-oz. can refried beans
1/2 c. salsa
13-oz. pkg. restaurant-style tortilla chips
1 1/2 c. shredded Monterey Jack cheese
1 1/2 c. shredded Cheddar cheese
pickled jalapeño slices, well drained
Optional: 1 c. guacamole, 1/2 c. sour cream
Garnish: chopped fresh cilantro, sliced ripe
    olives, shredded lettuce, additional salsa

Sauté onion and garlic in hot oil in a skillet over medium heat 4 to 5 minutes or until onion is tender. Add beans and salsa to pan, stirring until beans are creamy. Cook one minute or until heated. Scatter most of chips on a parchment paper-lined large baking sheet or an oven-proof platter. Top with bean mixture, cheeses and desired amount of jalapeños. Bake at 450 degrees for 8 minutes or until cheeses melt and edges are golden. Top with small dollops of guacamole and sour cream, if desired. Add desired toppings. Serve hot.

Vickie , *Gooseberry Patch*

Butternut Squash Soup

A creamy, flavorful soup that is perfect to start a holiday meal.

Makes 8 cups

3-lb. butternut squash
8 carrots, peeled and cut intopieces
2 1/2 c. chicken broth
3/4 c. orange juice
1/2 t. salt
1/2 t. ground ginger
1/2 c. whipping cream
Optional: 2 T. finely chopped toasted pecans
    and nutmeg

Cut squash in half lengthwise; remove seeds. Place squash, cut-sides down, in a shallow pan; add hot water to pan to a depth of 3/4 inch. Cover with aluminum foil and bake at 400 degrees for 40 minutes or until tender; drain. Scoop out pulp; mash. Discard shell. Cook carrots in boiling water 25 minutes or until tender; drain and mash. Combine squash, carrots, chicken broth and next 3 ingredients in a bowl. Process half of mixture in a food processor or blender until smooth. Repeat procedure with remaining half of squash mixture. Place puréed mixture in a large saucepan; bring to a simmer. Stir in cream; return to a simmer. Remove from heat. To serve, ladle into individual bowls. Garnish with pecans and nutmeg, if desired.

Butternut Squash Soup

Jackie Balla, *Walbridge, OH*

Green Bean Delight

An old standby dressed up with shredded cheese and nuts.

Serves 8 to 10

4 16-oz. cans green beans, drained
1-oz. pkg. ranch salad dressing mix
2 10¾-oz. cans cream of mushroom soup
¼ c. milk
8-oz. pkg. shredded Colby Jack cheese
1 c. sliced almonds or cashews
2.8-oz. can French fried onions

Spread green beans in a lightly greased 13"x9" baking pan; set aside. Combine salad dressing mix, soup and milk in a bowl; drizzle over beans. Sprinkle with cheese, nuts and onions. Bake, uncovered, at 350 degrees for 25 minutes.

Etha Hutchcroft, *Ames, IA*

Cornbread Dressing

This Southern classic is a Thanksgiving dinner favorite. This version is quite moist; if you prefer a firmer dressing, use only 4 cans of broth.

Serves 16 to 18

1 c. butter, divided
3 c. white cornmeal
1 c. all-purpose flour
2 T. sugar
2 t. baking powder
1½ t. salt
1 t. baking soda
7 eggs, divided
3 c. buttermilk
3 c. soft bread crumbs
3 c. celery, finely chopped
2 c. onion, finely chopped
½ c. fresh sage, finely chopped or 1 T. dried sage
5 10½-oz. cans chicken broth
1 T. pepper

Place ½ cup butter in a 13"x9" baking pan; heat in oven at 425 degrees for 4 minutes. Combine cornmeal and next 5 ingredients; whisk in 3 eggs and buttermilk. Pour hot butter from pan into batter, stirring until blended. Pour batter into pan. Bake at 425 degrees for 30 minutes or until golden. Cool. Crumble cornbread into a large bowl; stir in bread crumbs and set aside. Melt remaining butter in a large skillet over medium heat; add celery and onion and sauté until tender. Stir in sage and sauté one more minute. Stir vegetables, remaining eggs, chicken broth and pepper into cornbread mixture; spoon into one lightly greased 13"x9" baking pan and one lightly greased 8"x8" baking pan. Cover and chill 8 hours, if desired. Bake dressing, uncovered, at 375 degrees for 35 to 40 minutes or until golden.

Cornbread Dressing

Laura Fuller, *Fort Wayne, IN*

Brussels Sprouts au Gratin

Brussels sprouts have never looked as good as they do smothered in this yummy cheese sauce and capped with crumbs. If you prefer, substitute regular Worcestershire sauce for the white wine variety.

Serves 8

¼ c. dry bread crumbs
1 T. grated Parmesan cheese
2 lbs. fresh Brussels sprouts, trimmed and
  halved lengthwise
2 T. butter
2 T. all-purpose flour
1½ c. milk
1 c. shredded Gruyère or Swiss cheese
1 T. white wine Worcestershire sauce
½ t. salt
¼ t. pepper
¼ t. paprika

Combine bread crumbs and Parmesan cheese; set aside. Cook Brussels sprouts in boiling water to cover 12 minutes or until barely tender. Drain and place in a lightly greased 1½-quart gratin dish or an 11"x7" baking pan. Set aside. Melt butter in a saucepan over low heat; add flour, stirring until smooth. Cook, stirring constantly, one minute. Gradually add milk; cook over medium heat, stirring constantly, until thickened and bubbly. Add Gruyère cheese and next 3 ingredients, stirring until cheese melts. Spoon sauce over Brussels sprouts; sprinkle with bread crumb mixture and paprika. Bake, uncovered, at 350 degrees for 20 minutes or until golden and bubbly.

Kendall Hale, *Lynn, MA*

Roast Turkey with Sage Butter

This roasted turkey is simply beautiful!

Serves 12

1 c. butter, softened
3 T. fresh sage, chopped
8 slices bacon, crisply cooked and crumbled
salt and pepper to taste
16-lb. turkey, thawed if frozen
3 c. leeks, chopped
8 sprigs fresh sage
3 bay leaves, crumbled
4 c. chicken broth, divided

Combine butter, sage and bacon; sprinkle with salt and pepper. Set aside. Remove giblets and neck from turkey; reserve for another use. Rinse turkey and pat dry. Sprinkle inside of turkey with salt and pepper; add leeks, sage and bay leaves. Loosen skin and spread ⅓ cup butter mixture over breast under skin. Place turkey on rack of a large broiler pan. Rub 2 tablespoons butter mixture over turkey. Set aside ⅓ cup mixture for gravy; reserve remaining mixture for basting. Pour ⅓ cup broth over turkey. Bake turkey at 350 degrees for 2½ hours or until a meat thermometer inserted into thigh registers 170 degrees. Baste every 30 minutes with ⅓ cup broth; brush occasionally with remaining butter mixture. Transfer turkey to a platter; keep warm. For gravy, pour juices and bits from pan into a large measuring cup. Spoon off fat and discard. Bring juices and 2 cups broth to a boil in a large saucepan; boil until liquid is reduced to 2 cups. Whisk in reserved ⅓ cup butter mixture. Season with pepper.

Roast Turkey with Sage Butter

Charlotte Weaver, *Purcell, OK*

Country Butterscotch Yams

For an extra treat, top with half of a 16-ounce package of marshmallows and return to the oven until lightly browned.

Serves 6

8 14-oz. yams, peeled, cut into 1/2-inch slices
    and boiled
1/2 c. corn syrup
1/2 c. brown sugar, packed
1/4 c. half-and-half
2 T. butter
1/2 t. salt
1/2 t. cinnamon

Arrange yams in an ungreased 13"x9" baking pan; bake at 325 degrees for 15 minutes. Combine remaining ingredients in a 2-quart saucepan; boil 5 minutes, stirring constantly. Pour over yams; bake 15 more minutes, basting often.

Rhonda Johnson, *Studio City, CA*

Bruschetta with Cranberry Relish

Serve these crisp, savory slices at your next Thanksgiving feast...you may just start a new tradition!

Makes 18 to 20 servings

1 French baguette loaf, sliced 1/4-inch thick
1 to 2 T. olive oil
1 t. orange zest
1 t. lemon zest
1/2 c. chopped pecans
1/2 c. crumbled blue cheese

Brush baguette slices lightly with oil. Arrange on a broiler pan; toast lightly under broiler. Turn slices over; spread with Cranberry Relish. Sprinkle with zests, pecans and blue cheese. Place under broiler just until cheese begins to melt.

CRANBERRY RELISH:

16-oz. can whole-berry cranberry sauce
6-oz. pkg. sweetened dried cranberries
1/2 c. sugar
1 t. rum extract
1 c. chopped pecans

Stir all ingredients together.

Bruschetta with Cranberry Relish

Sandy Kelley, *West Salem, WI*

Cranberry Relish Salad

This salad is softly set and can be spooned out as a relish or cut into squares and served over lettuce leaves.

Serves 10

2 c. boiling water
2 3-oz. pkgs. cherry gelatin mix
¾ c. sugar
3 Red Delicious apples, peeled, cored and
    quartered
3 navel oranges, peeled and sectioned
1 c. pecan halves, toasted
12-oz. pkg. fresh or frozen cranberries
8-oz. can crushed pineapple

Stir boiling water into gelatin mix in a lightly greased 13"x9" baking pan until gelatin mix is completely dissolved. Add sugar, stirring until completely dissolved. Process apples and oranges in a food processor until chopped; stir into gelatin mixture. Process pecans and cranberries in food processor until chopped; stir into apple mixture. Drain pineapple in a wire mesh strainer, pressing out juice with the back of a spoon; reserve juice for another use. Add drained pineapple to cranberry mixture, stirring until fruit and nuts are thoroughly distributed in gelatin mixture. Cover and chill 8 hours. Spoon out as a relish or cut into squares.

Fern Bruner, *Phoenix, AZ*

Bacon–Brown Sugar Brussels Sprouts

A delicious way to get your family to enjoy eating this leafy veggie!

Serves 6 to 8

4 slices bacon
14-oz. can chicken broth
1 T. brown sugar, packed
1 t. salt
1½ lbs. Brussels sprouts, trimmed and halved

Cook bacon in a Dutch oven over medium heat for 10 minutes, or until crisp. Remove bacon and drain on paper towels, reserving drippings in pan. Add chicken broth, brown sugar and salt to reserved drippings; bring to a boil. Stir in Brussels sprouts. Cover and cook for 6 to 8 minutes , until tender. Transfer to a serving bowl using a slotted spoon; sprinkle with crumbled bacon. Serve immediately.

Bacon-Brown Sugar Brussels Sprouts

Layna Jarrett, *Pennsboro, WV*

Nutty Sausage & Cranberry Stuffing

Whether you call it stuffing or dressing, we think this recipe is scrumptious.

Serves 8 to 10

16-oz. pkg. cornbread stuffing mix
2 c. chicken broth
1 egg, beaten
½ c. butter, divided
1 c. onion, chopped
1 c. celery, chopped
1 c. ground Italian pork sausage, browned and drained
1 c. sweetened dried cranberries
½ c. chopped pecans

Prepare stuffing mix according to package directions, using broth, egg and ¼ cup butter; set aside. Sauté onion and celery in remaining butter until translucent. Stir onion mixture and remaining ingredients into stuffing; toss well to coat. Spread mixture in a lightly greased 13"x9" baking pan. Cover and bake at 350 degrees for 30 minutes.

Jodi Zarnoth-Hirsch, *Chilton, WI*

Cranberry Meatloaves

This favorite comfort food recipe is dressed up a bit for the holidays with a little cranberry topping.

Serves 5

1 lb. lean ground beef
1 c. cooked rice
½ c. tomato juice
¼ c. onion, minced
1 egg
1 t. salt
16-oz. can whole-berry cranberry sauce
⅓ c. brown sugar, packed
1 T. lemon juice

Mix together ground beef, rice, tomato juice, onion, egg and salt. Shape mixture evenly into 5 mini meatloaves and place in a greased 13"x9" baking pan. Mix together cranberry sauce, brown sugar and lemon juice; spoon over top of each loaf. Bake at 350 degrees for 45 minutes.

Cranberry Meatloaves

Nola Coons, *Gooseberry Patch*

Cranberry Tea

A special treat for tea lovers. So yummy with cranberry scones!

Makes 4 quarts

6 c. water, divided
2 family-size or 8 regular teabags
1 t. whole cloves
2 2½-inch cinnamon sticks
2 c. sugar
2 c. cranberry juice cocktail
1 c. orange juice
¼ c. lemon juice

In a large pot, bring 4 cups water to a boil. Add teabags, cloves and cinnamon sticks; cover and steep for 5 minutes. Strain, discarding teabags and spices. Stir in remaining water and other ingredients. Stir until sugar is dissolved. Serve warm or over ice.

Rogene Rogers, *Bemidji, MN*

Perfect Pecan Pie

Everyone looks forward to dessert, and this beautiful pie will not disappoint!

Serves 6

3 eggs
½ c. sugar
¼ t. salt
3 T. butter, melted
1 c. dark corn syrup
1 t. vanilla extract
9-inch pie crust
2 c. pecan halves
Optional: vanilla ice cream

Whisk together eggs and next 5 ingredients until thoroughly blended. Stir in pecans. Fit pie crust into a 9" pie plate according to package directions. Fold edges under and crimp. Pour filling into pie crust. Bake at 350 degrees on lower rack 40 minutes or until pie is set, covering edges with aluminum foil after 15 minutes. Cool completely on a wire rack. Serve with vanilla ice cream, if desired.

Perfect Pecan Pie

Sonna Johnson, *Goldfield, IA*

Roasted Sweet Potato Salad

Serve this salad chilled or at room temperature. Tossed in rosemary-honey vinaigrette, these golden potatoes come alive with flavor.

Serves 6 to 8

4 sweet potatoes, peeled and cubed
2 T. olive oil, divided
¼ c. honey
3 T. white wine vinegar
2 T. fresh rosemary, chopped
½ t. salt
½ t. pepper
2 cloves garlic, minced
Optional: fresh rosemary sprig

Coat a large roasting pan with non-stick vegetable spray; toss together potatoes and one tablespoon oil in pan. Bake, uncovered, at 450 degrees for 45 to 55 minutes or until potatoes are tender and roasted, stirring after 20 minutes. Whisk together remaining oil, honey and next 5 ingredients. Transfer warm potatoes to a large serving bowl; add dressing and toss gently. Cool. Garnish with a fresh rosemary sprig, if desired.

Vickie, *Gooseberry Patch*

Sweet Potato Cornbread

This rich cornbread is sure to become your family favorite. Baking it in a skillet makes the edges so wonderfully golden brown. Serve it with honey butter or raspberry jam.

Makes 6 servings

2 c. self-rising cornmeal mix
¼ c. sugar
1 t. cinnamon
1½ c. milk
1 c. cooked sweet potato, mashed
¼ c. butter, melted
1 egg, beaten

Whisk together all ingredients just until dry ingredients are moistened. Spoon batter into a greased 8" cast-iron skillet or pan. Bake at 425 degrees for 30 minutes or until a toothpick inserted in center comes out clean.

Sweet Potato Cornbread

Maria Temple, *New York, NY*

Sugar-Topped Muffins

Enjoy these warm muffins for a real treat!

Makes 2 dozen

18¼-oz. pkg. white cake mix
1 c. milk
2 eggs
½ t. nutmeg
⅓ c. sugar
½ t. cinnamon
¼ c. butter, melted

Blend cake mix, milk, eggs and nutmeg at low speed with an electric mixer until just moistened; beat at high speed 2 minutes. Fill paper-lined muffin cups ⅔ full. Bake at 350 degrees until golden, about 15 to 18 minutes. Cool 5 minutes. Combine sugar and cinnamon on a small plate. Brush muffin tops with butter; roll in sugar and cinnamon mixture. Serve warm.

Wendy Jacobs, *Idaho Falls, ID*

Tangy Turkey Salad Croissants

The day after Thanksgiving, my mom, sisters and I decided we wanted more than just the usual turkey sandwich. We combined some of our favorite flavors and came up with these turkey croissant sandwiches. We love them!

Makes 6 sandwiches

2 c. cooked turkey breast, cubed
1 orange, peeled and chopped
½ c. cranberries, finely chopped
½ c. mayonnaise
½ t. salt
¼ c. chopped pecans
6 croissants, split
Garnish: lettuce leaves

Combine turkey, orange, cranberries, mayonnaise and salt; chill. Stir in pecans before serving. Top each croissant half with ½ cup turkey mixture and a lettuce leaf. Top with remaining croissant half.

Tangy Turkey Salad Croissants

Kendall Hale, *Lynn, MA*

Whole Acorn Squash Cream Soup

This unique recipe celebrates the beauty of squash by using it as a serving bowl. Choose squash that stand upright for ease in baking and serving.

Serves 4

4 acorn squash
¼ c. cream cheese
1 c. whipping cream
1 c. chicken broth
½ t. salt
1 t. cinnamon

Cut off about one inch of stem ends of squash to reveal seeds. Scoop out and discard seeds and pulp. Arrange squash in a 13"x9" baking pan. Place one tablespoon cream cheese in each squash. Pour ¼ cup each cream and chicken broth over cream cheese in each squash; sprinkle each with ⅛ teaspoon salt and ¼ teaspoon cinnamon. Add water to baking pan to a depth of ½ inch. Bake, uncovered, at 350 degrees for one hour and 45 minutes or until squash are very tender. To serve, carefully set each squash in a shallow soup bowl.

Robyn Fiedler, *Tacoma, WA*

Turkey-Vegetable Chowder

This is a terrific, hearty chowder made using your leftover turkey!

Makes 8 cups

¼ c. butter
2 onions, chopped
2 T. all-purpose flour
1 t. curry powder
3 c. chicken broth
1 potato, peeled and chopped
1 c. carrots, peeled and thinly sliced
1 c. celery, thinly sliced
2 T. fresh parsley, minced
½ t. dried sage or poultry seasoning
3 c. cooked turkey, chopped
1½ c. half-and-half
10-oz. pkg. frozen chopped spinach
Optional: fresh parsley leaves

Melt butter in a small Dutch oven. Add onions and sauté 10 minutes. Stir in flour and curry powder. Cook 2 minutes. Add broth, potato, carrots, celery, parsley and sage. Reduce heat to low. Cover and simmer 10 to 15 minutes. Add turkey, half-and-half and frozen spinach. Cover and simmer, stirring occasionally, 10 minutes or until heated through. Garnish with fresh parsley leaves, if desired.

Turkey-Vegetable Chowder

Dana Thompson, *Delaware, OH*

Quick & Easy Veggie Salad

A simple, healthy choice to pair with any main dish...or serve it by itself with crunchy bread.

Serves 4

½ **head cauliflower, chopped**
1 **bunch broccoli, chopped**
1 **tomato, chopped**
¼ **red onion, sliced**
3 **to 4 T. Italian salad dressing**

Combine cauliflower, broccoli, tomato and onion in a serving bowl. Toss with dressing to taste.

Nancy Marti, *Edwardsville, IL*

Tasty Turkey Roll-Ups

A family favorite that's ready to serve in a jiffy! It's at the top of the request list whenever I ask for dinner suggestions. Serve with a side of steamed vegetables for a delicious meal.

Makes 4 to 6 servings

6-oz. **pkg. sage-flavored stuffing mix**
6 **to 8 thin slices deli roast turkey**
12-oz. **jar turkey gravy**

Prepare stuffing mix according to package directions. Take one slice of turkey and put 2 tablespoons of stuffing on one end. Roll up turkey slice, beginning at the end with the stuffing; secure with a toothpick. Continue until all turkey slices are filled and rolled. Place rolls in a lightly greased 8"x8" baking pan, seam-side down. Spread any extra stuffing around rolls; top with gravy. Bake, uncovered, at 350 degrees for 20 to 30 minutes, until heated through.

Brandi Glenn, *Los Osos, CA*

Gobblin' Good Turkey Burgers

Ground turkey is spiced up a bit with Italian seasonings and Worcestershire sauce. Yum!

Makes 4 to 6 sandwiches

1 lb. **ground turkey**
2 T. **fresh chives, chopped**
½ c. **Italian-flavored dry bread crumbs**
¼ c. **Worcestershire sauce**
½ t. **dry mustard**
salt and pepper to taste
4 **to 6 hamburger buns, split**

Combine all ingredients except buns; form into 4 to 6 patties. Grill to desired doneness; serve on hamburger buns.

Gobblin' Good Turkey Burgers

Barbara Hoover, *Des Moines, IA*

Pumpkin Pie Ice Cream Fantasy

Two holiday dessert classics are swirled with caramel and pecans...what's not to love?

Serves 12

1 baked pumpkin pie
½ gal. vanilla ice cream
caramel topping
pecan halves, toasted

Place pie in freezer one hour; remove pie from freezer and chop pie into one-inch pieces. Allow ice cream to stand 8 to 10 minutes to slightly soften. Spoon ice cream into a large bowl. Gently fold in pie pieces until blended. To serve, scoop each serving into a wine glass or dessert bowl. Drizzle with caramel topping and top with pecans.

Della Feist, *Faith, SD*

Cranberry-Orange Warmer

This is a favorite drink around our home during the fall and winter holidays. Make a double batch and invite friends over.

Makes 20 servings

16-oz. pkg. frozen cranberries, thawed
4-inch cinnamon stick
8 c. water
6-oz. can frozen orange juice concentrate, thawed
6-oz. can frozen lemonade concentrate, thawed
1 c. sugar

In a saucepan, bring cranberries, cinnamon stick and water to a boil. Boil for 5 minutes. Strain, discarding cranberries and cinnamon stick. Return juice to saucepan. Add juice concentrates and sugar to saucepan; stir until sugar dissolves. Serve warm.

Cranberry-Orange Warmer

Sarah Lundvall, *Ephrata, PA*

Cranberry Hootycreek Pancakes

This is my take on a favorite cookie recipe... for breakfast. My 2-year-old gobbles them up faster than I can make them.

Serves 4

1/2 c. all-purpose flour
1/2 c. quick-cooking oats, uncooked
1 T. sugar
1 t. baking powder
1/2 t. baking soda
1/2 t. salt
1 t. vanilla extract
3/4 c. buttermilk
2 T. oil
1 egg, beaten
1/2 c. white chocolate chips
1/2 c. sweetened dried cranberries

In a bowl, mix flour, oats, sugar, baking powder, baking soda and salt. Add vanilla, buttermilk, oil and egg; stir until well blended. Stir in white chocolate chips and cranberries. In a large, lightly greased griddle over medium heat, drop batter by 1/4 cupfuls. Cook for about 3 minutes, until tops start to form bubbles. Flip and cook 2 additional minutes, or until both sides are golden.

Leslie Williams, *Americus, GA*

Maple-Pecan Brunch Ring

A sweet & simple way to make a tasty treat for holiday guests.

Makes about 12 servings

3/4 c. chopped pecans
1/2 c. brown sugar, packed
2 t. cinnamon
2 17.3-oz. tubes refrigerated jumbo flaky biscuits
2 T. butter, melted
1/2 c. maple syrup

Combine pecans, brown sugar and cinnamon; set aside. Split each biscuit horizontally; brush half of the biscuits with butter and sprinkle with half the pecan mixture. Arrange topped biscuits in a circle on an ungreased baking sheet; overlap each biscuit slightly and keep within 2 inches of the edge of the baking sheet. Brush remaining biscuit halves with butter; sprinkle with remaining pecan mixture. Arrange a second ring just inside the first ring, overlapping edges. Bake at 350 degrees for 30 to 35 minutes, until golden. Remove to wire rack; cool 10 minutes. Brush with maple syrup.

Maple-Pecan Brunch Ring

Linda Corcoran, *Metuchen, NJ*

Maple-Topped Sweet Potato Skins

I love finding these appetizers on a buffet table...they're absolutely wonderful!

Makes one dozen

6 sweet potatoes
½ c. cream cheese, softened
¼ c. sour cream
2 t. cinnamon, divided
2 t. nutmeg, divided
2 t. ground ginger, divided
2 c. chopped walnuts or pecans
3 T. butter, softened
¼ c. brown sugar, packed
Garnish: warm maple syrup, additional nuts

Pierce potatoes with a fork. Bake at 400 degrees or microwave on high setting until tender; cool. Slice each potato in half lengthwise; scoop out baked insides, keeping skins intact. Place potato skins on an ungreased baking sheet. Mash baked potato in a bowl until smooth; add cream cheese, sour cream and one teaspoon each of spices. Mix well and spoon into potato skins. In a bowl, mix nuts, butter, brown sugar and remaining spices; sprinkle over top. Bake at 400 degrees for 15 minutes. Drizzle with warm maple syrup; garnish as desired.

Tamara Aherns, *Sparta, MI*

Tamara's Pickled Beets

Grandma knew how to keep fresh beets from staining her hands while cutting them. She rubbed her hands with vegetable oil first. I love to make these to serve with our Thanksgiving turkey. So yummy!

Serves 4 to 6

⅓ c. sugar
⅓ c. red wine vinegar
⅓ c. water
½ t. cinnamon
¼ t. salt
¼ t. ground cloves
5 whole peppercorns
2 c. red or golden beets, peeled, cooked and sliced, or 16-oz. can sliced beets, drained

Combine all ingredients except beets in a saucepan over medium-high heat. Bring to a boil, stirring constantly. Add beets and return to a boil. Reduce heat and simmer, covered, 5 minutes. Let cool and chill for 4 hours to overnight before serving. Store in refrigerator.

Tamara's Pickled Beets

Chapter Two

Winter Celebrations

Experience all the joy that winter holidays bring with delightful recipes that you create for your family & friends. Bake hearty Christmas Breakfast Stratas for the entire family as you celebrate Christmas morning, and then create an elegant Tuscan Pork Loin for dinner on the big day. Have a special sweetheart? Stir up some Be Mine Cherry Brownies and 2-Kiss Cupcakes to make the day perfect. Then warm them up with sweet Cherry Cobbler for those cold February holidays. You'll love celebrating the season with the all-time-favorite recipes you find in this collection of best-loved winter recipes.

Vickie, *Gooseberry Patch*

Emily's Gingerbread Cookies

This came from my daughter Emily's elementary class assignment. She unscrambled words to uncover the recipe... she wrote "flower" instead of "flour." I still have the paper and treasure it!

Makes 2 dozen

¹⁄₃ c. brown sugar, packed
¹⁄₃ c. shortening
²⁄₃ c molasses
1 egg, beaten
3 c. all-purpose flour
1 T. baking powder
1½ t. ground ginger
½ t. salt
Optional: small candies or sprinkles

Blend together brown sugar and shortening until light and fluffy. Beat in molasses. Add egg, beating well, In a separate bowl, sift together flour, baking powder, ginger and salt. Add flour mixture to sugar mixture; mix well. Cover and refrigerate for 2 hours. Divide dough into fourths. Roll out to ¼-inch thickness. Cut with cookie cutters. Place on greased baking sheets. Bake at 350 degrees for 5 to 7 minutes, until dark golden. Cool slightly on pans before removing to wire racks to cool completely. Decorate as desired.

FROSTING:

4½ c. powdered sugar
6 T. butter, melted
6 T. milk
2 T. vanilla extract
1 T. lemon juice
Optional: few drops food coloring

Combine all ingredients in a medium bowl. Beat with an electric mixer on low speed until smooth.

Emily's Gingerbread Cookies

Julia Leone, *Fairport, NY*

Christmas Crunch

This sweet mix looks oh-so pretty in jars for gift-giving. Just cover the lids with fabric, then tie on a ribbon and a tiny ornament.

Makes about 16 cups

3 c. doughnut-shaped oat cereal
3 c. bite-size crispy corn cereal squares
3 c. bite-size crispy rice cereal squares
2 c. salted peanuts
12-oz. pkg. candy-coated chocolates
1½ lbs. white melting chocolate disks

Combine all ingredients except melting chocolate in a very large bowl; set aside. Place chocolate in a microwave-safe bowl. Microwave on high for 2 to 3 minutes, stirring every minute, until melted and smooth. Pour melted chocolate over cereal mixture; stir gently to coat. Pour out onto wax paper; let harden. Break into pieces; store in airtight containers.

Valarie Dennard, *Palatka, FL*

Chocolate Eggnog

A great no-fuss recipe for jazzing up store-bought eggnog.

Makes 3 quarts

2 qts. eggnog
16-oz. can chocolate syrup
Optional: ½ c. light rum
1 c. whipping cream
2 T. powdered sugar
Garnish: baking cocoa

Combine eggnog, chocolate syrup and rum, if using, in a punch bowl, stirring well. Beat whipping cream with an electric mixer on high speed until foamy. Add powdered sugar; continue beating until stiff peaks form. Dollop whipped cream over eggnog; sift cocoa over top. Serve immediately.

> ⟋ **Holiday Helper** ⟍
>
> Make cookies, cereal mix and other holiday treats ahead of time and freeze in airtight containers. When the holiday is near, you will have more time to celebrate with family & friends.

Chocolate Eggnog

Sandi Boothman, *Camden, MI*

Graham Pralines

A friend gave me this easy recipe. It is wonderful for the holidays. Try cinnamon grahams too...yum!

Makes about 2 dozen

1 sleeve graham crackers
½ c. butter
½ c. margarine
1 c. brown sugar, packed
⅛ t. salt
1 c. chopped pecans

Cover a baking sheet with aluminum foil; spray lightly with non-stick vegetable spray. Break crackers and arrange on baking sheet; set aside. Melt butter, margarine, sugar and salt together in a saucepan over low heat. Bring to a boil and boil for 2 minutes; pour over crackers. Sprinkle pecans over top; bake at 350 degrees for 10 to 12 minutes. Let cool; break apart.

Beckie Apple, *Grannis, AR*

Chocolate Granola Brittle

The beauty of this recipe is that you can make a decadent brittle in the microwave in half the time it takes to make the traditional candy.

Makes about one pound

1 c. sugar
½ c. light corn syrup
⅛ t. salt
1 c. pecans, coarsely chopped
1 T. butter
1 t. vanilla extract
1 t. baking soda
¾ c. chocolate granola
3 1-oz. sqs. semi-sweet baking chocolate
1½ T. shortening

Combine first 3 ingredients in a 2-quart glass bowl. Microwave on high 5 minutes. Stir in pecans. Microwave 1½ minutes. Stir in butter and vanilla. Microwave one minute and 45 seconds or until candy is the color of peanut butter. Stir in baking soda (mixture will bubble). Quickly pour candy onto a lightly greased rimless baking sheet. (Pour as thinly as possible without spreading candy.) Cover brittle quickly with parchment paper and use a rolling pin to thin out candy; peel off parchment. Sprinkle granola over brittle. Replace parchment and use rolling pin to press granola into brittle; peel off parchment. Cool brittle completely; break into pieces. Place chocolate squares and shortening in a small bowl. Microwave on high, 1½ to 2 minutes, stirring after one minute. Dip each piece of brittle halfway into chocolate mixture. Place dipped brittle on parchment paper to harden. Store in an airtight container.

Chocolate Granola Brittle

Georgia Muth, *Penn Valley, CA*

Cranberry-Pecan Coffee Cakes

These tender cranberry-and-nut streusel loaves are sure to please friends and neighbors.

Makes 4 mini coffee cakes

½ c. butter, softened
1 c. sugar
2 eggs
2 c. all-purpose flour
2 t. baking powder
½ t. baking soda
½ t. salt
8-oz. container sour cream
1 t. almond extract
1 t. vanilla extract
16-oz. can whole-berry cranberry sauce
1 c. coarsely chopped pecans

Beat butter at medium speed with an electric mixer until creamy. Gradually add sugar, beating well. Add eggs, one at a time, beating until blended after each addition. Combine flour and next 3 ingredients. Add flour mixture to butter mixture alternately with sour cream, beginning and ending with flour mixture. Stir in extracts. Spoon ½ cup batter into each of 4 greased and floured 5"x3" mini loaf pans. Gently stir cranberry sauce; spoon 3 tablespoons over batter in each pan and spread lightly to edges. Sprinkle 2 tablespoons pecans over cranberry sauce in each pan. Repeat layers in each pan using remaining batter, cranberry sauce and pecans. Bake at 350 degrees for 48 to 50 minutes or until a toothpick inserted in center comes out clean. Cool in pans on a wire rack 15 minutes; remove from pans and let cool completely. Drizzle Almond Cream Glaze over cooled cakes.

ALMOND CREAM GLAZE:

¾ c. powdered sugar
2 T. whipping cream
½ t. almond extract

Stir together all ingredients. Makes ⅓ cup.

⌐ Holiday Helper ⌐

Keep food-safe cellophane bags on hand to wrap up baked goods for holiday gifts. Slide the goodie in the bag and tie with a piece of torn fabric or red ribbon.

Cranberry-Pecan Coffee Cakes

Vickie, *Gooseberry Patch*

Ginger Scones

Top these yummy scones with sweetened whipped cream!

Makes 8 scones

2¾ c. all-purpose flour
2 t. baking powder
½ t. salt
½ c. sugar
¾ c. butter
⅓ c. crystallized ginger, chopped
1 c. milk

Combine first 4 ingredients in a large bowl; cut butter into flour mixture with a pastry blender until crumbly. Stir in ginger. Add milk, stirring just until dry ingredients are moistened. Turn dough out onto a lightly floured surface and knead 10 to 15 times. Pat or roll dough to ¾-inch thickness; shape into a round and cut dough into 8 wedges. Place wedges on a lightly greased baking sheet. Bake at 400 degrees for 18 to 22 minutes or until scones are barely golden. Cool slightly on a wire rack.

Diana Hamilton, *Beaverton, OR*

Good Neighbor Sugar Cookies

These are the best sugar cookies ever!

Makes 3 dozen

3 c. all-purpose flour
1 t. cream of tartar
1 t. baking soda
1 t. salt
¾ c. butter
2 eggs, beaten
1 c. sugar
1 t. vanilla extract
Optional: candy sprinkles or decorations

Mix together flour, cream of tartar, baking soda and salt in a bowl. In a separate bowl, whisk together remaining ingredients with a fork. Stir butter mixture into flour mixture. Wrap dough in plastic wrap; refrigerate for 30 minutes. On a floured surface, roll out dough ⅛-inch thick; cut out with cookie cutters. Arrange on lightly greased baking sheets. Bake at 375 degrees for 5 to 6 minutes, until lightly golden. Cool. Frost using one tablespoon of frosting per cookie. Decorate as desired.

SUGAR COOKIE FROSTING:
5 c. powdered sugar
5½ to 6½ T. water
1½ t. almond extract
paste food coloring

Combine powdered sugar, water and almond extract in a medium bowl; beat until smooth. Transfer frosting into small bowls and tint with food coloring. Spread onto cooled cookies.

Good Neighbor Sugar Cookies

Karen Whitby, *Charlotte, VT*

Christmas Rainbow Cake

For a festive touch, roll out green and red gumdrops and then cut them to resemble holly leaves and berries.

Serves 6 to 8

18½-oz. pkg. moist white cake mix
3-oz. pkg. raspberry gelatin mix
2 c. boiling water, divided
3-oz. pkg. lime gelatin mix
12-oz. container frozen whipped topping, thawed

Prepare cake mix and bake in 2 greased 8" round cake pans, according to package directions. Cool in pans 10 minutes; remove from pans and cool completely on wire racks. Clean pans and return cake layers, top sides up, to pans; pierce each layer with a fork every half-inch. In a small bowl, combine raspberry gelatin mix and one cup boiling water, stirring until gelatin dissolves; pour raspberry gelatin over one layer. In another small bowl, combine lime gelatin mix and remaining one cup boiling water, stirring until gelatin dissolves; pour lime gelatin over second layer. Chill layers 3 to 4 hours. Dip one cake pan into a pan of warm water to loosen cake; invert onto a plate and remove pan. Spread one cup whipped topping on top of layer. Dip second cake pan into warm water, invert on top of first layer and remove pan. Spread remaining topping on top and sides of cake.

Peggy Cummings, *Cibolo, TX*

Christmas Peppermint & Chocolate Meringues

Use the ice pulse button on your blender to make quick work of crushing the candies.

Makes 3 dozen

2 egg whites
⅛ t. cream of tartar
⅛ t. salt
¾ c. sugar
½ t. vanilla extract
3 T. peppermint candies, crushed
2 c. mini semi-sweet chocolate chips

In a large bowl, beat egg whites with an electric mixer at high speed until foamy. Add cream of tartar and salt, beating until mixed. Gradually add sugar, one tablespoon at a time, beating well after each addition until stiff peaks form. Gently fold in remaining ingredients. Drop by teaspoonfuls 1½ inches apart on baking sheets sprayed with non-stick vegetable spray. Bake at 250 degrees for 40 minutes, or until dry. Remove to wire racks to cool completely. Store in an airtight container.

Christmas Peppermint & Chocolate Meringues

Thais Menges, *Three Rivers, MI*

Grandma Miller's Nutmeg Logs

You'll want more than just one!

Makes 4 dozen

1 c. butter, softened
¾ c. sugar
1 egg, lightly beaten
2 t. vanilla extract
2 t. rum extract
1 t. nutmeg
3 c. all-purpose flour
Garnish: additional nutmeg

In a large bowl, blend together butter and sugar. Stir in egg and extracts. Add nutmeg and flour; mix well. Divide dough into 4 portions. Roll each portion into a long rope; cut into 1½-inch lengths. Place on ungreased baking sheets. Bake at 350 degrees for 10 to 15 minutes. Cool on wire racks. Spread Frosting on cookies. Run the tines of a fork across frosting to resemble a log. Sprinkle lightly with nutmeg.

FROSTING:

3 T. butter, softened
½ t. vanilla extract
1 t. rum extract
2½ c. powdered sugar
3 T. milk

Combine butter, extracts and powdered sugar. Blend in milk to desired consistency.

Jennifer Martineau, *Delaware, OH*

Candy Cane Thumbprints

My little daughter insists on making the thumbprints herself...won't Santa love finding a plate of these cookies on Christmas Eve!

Makes about 3 dozen

⅔ c. butter, softened
½ c. sugar
¼ t. salt
1 egg, beaten
1 t. vanilla extract
1½ c. all-purpose flour
Garnish: crushed peppermint candies

With an electric mixer on low speed, blend butter, sugar and salt. Mix in egg and vanilla. Beat in as much flour as possible; stir in remaining flour. Cover; chill for one hour. Shape dough into one-inch balls; place 2 inches apart on ungreased baking sheets. Bake at 375 degrees for 8 to 10 minutes, until lightly golden around edges. Remove from oven; make a thumbprint in each cookie with thumb. Cool. Pipe Filling into centers; sprinkle with crushed candy.

FILLING:

¼ c. butter, softened
¼ t. peppermint extract
1½ c. powdered sugar
2 to 3 t. milk

Blend butter and extract. Gradually add powdered sugar and milk to a piping consistency.

Candy Cane Thumbprints

Vickie, *Gooseberry Patch*

Jumbo Chocolate Cupcakes

You can never have enough chocolate!

Makes one dozen

1 c. butter, softened
½ c. sugar
1 c. light brown sugar, packed
4 eggs
3 1-oz. sqs. unsweetened baking chocolate, melted
3 1-oz. sqs. semi-sweet baking chocolate, melted
1 t. vanilla extract
2 c. all-purpose flour
1 t. baking soda
½ t. salt
1 c. buttermilk
12 Christmas-themed cupcake toppers

Beat butter at medium speed with an electric mixer until creamy. Gradually add sugars, beating well. Add eggs, one at a time, beating after each addition. Add melted chocolates and vanilla, beating well. Combine flour, baking soda and salt; add to batter alternately with buttermilk, beginning and ending with flour mixture. Beat at low speed after each addition until blended. Spoon batter into paper-lined jumbo muffin cups, filling ¾ full. Bake at 350 degrees for 30 minutes or until a toothpick inserted in center comes out clean. Cool in pans on wire racks 5 minutes. Remove from pans and cool completely on wire racks 45 minutes. Spread with Thick Chocolate Frosting. Insert one topper into top of each cupcake.

THICK CHOCOLATE FROSTING:

½ c. butter, softened
16-oz. pkg. powdered sugar
1 c. semi-sweet chocolate chips, melted
½ c. whipping cream
2 t. vanilla extract
⅛ t. salt

Beat butter at medium speed with an electric mixer until creamy; gradually add powdered sugar alternately with melted chocolate and whipping cream. Beat at low speed after each addition until blended. Stir in vanilla and salt. Makes 3½ cups.

Francie Stutzman, *Dalton, Ohio*

Mrs. Claus' Christmas Bread

Packed with delicious fruit and nuts...share a loaf with a friend!

Makes one loaf

1 c. sugar
2 T. butter, softened
1 egg, beaten
2 c. all-purpose flour
1 t. baking powder
½ t. baking soda
½ t. salt
¾ c. orange juice
1 c. cranberries, chopped
½ c. chopped pecans

Blend sugar, butter and egg together in a large bowl. Add remaining ingredients; mix well and pour into a greased 9"x5" loaf pan. Bake at 350 degrees for 45 to 50 minutes.

Mrs. Claus' Christmas Bread

Rebecca Ferguson, *Carlisle. AR*

Homemade Eggnog

There's nothing like the taste of homemade eggnog at holiday time!

Serves 12

²/₃ c. sugar
4 egg yolks
½ t. salt
4 c. milk
2 qts. half-and-half
nutmeg to taste
1 pt. whipping cream, chilled
3 T. sugar
2 t. vanilla extract
Optional: frozen whipped topping, thawed, and cinnamon or nutmeg

Beat sugar into egg yolks in a saucepan; add salt and stir in milk. Cook mixture over medium heat, stirring constantly, until mixture coats the back of a metal spoon. Remove from heat and set pan in ice water to cool quickly. Pour through a sieve to remove lumps. Add half-and-half to cooled mixture; sprinkle with nutmeg. In a separate bowl, whip cream with sugar and vanilla; fold into egg mixture. Stir well before serving. Garnish with a dollop of whipped topping and a sprinkle of cinnamon or nutmeg, if desired.

Bobbi Carney, *Hobart, IN*

Peppermint Candy Cheesecake

Drizzle strawberry syrup on each slice right before serving for a merry little touch.

Serves 12

1 c. graham cracker crumbs
¾ c. sugar, divided
6 T. butter, melted and divided
1½ c. sour cream
2 eggs
1 T. all-purpose flour
2 t. vanilla extract
2 8-oz. pkgs. cream cheese, softened
¼ c. peppermint candies, coarsely crushed
Optional: frozen whipped topping, thawed; crushed peppermint candies

Blend crumbs, ¼ cup sugar and ¼ cup melted butter in bottom of an ungreased 8" round springform pan; press evenly over bottom. Blend sour cream, remaining sugar, eggs, flour and vanilla in a blender or food processor until smooth, stopping to scrape sides. Add cream cheese and blend; stir in remaining melted butter until completely smooth. Fold in crushed candies and pour over crust. Bake at 325 degrees for 45 minutes. Remove from oven and run a knife around edge of pan. Cool, then refrigerate overnight. Loosen pan sides and remove springform; serve garnished with whipped topping and crushed candies, if desired.

Peppermint Candy Cheesecake

Teresa Beal, *Bowling Green, KY*

Filet Mignon with Mushrooms

This upscale dish is my family's favorite Christmas dinner.

Serves 4

1 T. oil
8-oz. pkg. sliced mushrooms
4 cloves garlic, minced
4 6-oz. beef tenderloin filets
½ t. salt
½ t. pepper
½ t. garlic powder
⅓ c. Marsala wine or beef broth

Pour oil into a large skillet; place over medium-high heat until hot. Add mushrooms and garlic; cook 5 minutes or until liquid evaporates, stirring frequently. Remove from heat. Meanwhile, sprinkle each filet with salt, pepper and garlic powder. Place the filets on a lightly greased rack in a broiler pan; broil 3 inches from heat 5 to 6 minutes on each side or to desired degree of doneness. Add wine or broth to mushroom mixture and bring to a boil; cook 2 minutes or until wine is almost absorbed. Place each filet on a serving plate and top with mushroom mixture.

Georgia Cooper, *Helena, MT*

Cranberry-Gorgonzola Green Salad

Tart dried cranberries and Gorgonzola contribute outstanding flavor and to this green salad. To add holiday color and variety, add half each of an unpeeled Granny Smith apple and your favorite crisp red apple.

Serves 8

⅓ c. oil
¼ c. seasoned rice vinegar
¾ t. Dijon mustard
1 clove garlic, pressed
1 small head Bibb lettuce, torn
1 small head green leaf lettuce, torn
1 apple, cored and chopped
⅓ c. coarsely chopped walnuts, toasted
⅓ c. sweetened dried cranberries
⅓ c. crumbled Gorgonzola cheese

Whisk together oil, vinegar, mustard and garlic in a small bowl; set aside. Just before serving, combine remaining ingredients in a large bowl. Pour dressing over salad; toss gently.

> ∼ **Simple Ingredient Swap** ∼
> If you're not a fan of Gorgonzola, try swapping it out with feta or a mild goat cheese.

Cranberry-Gorgonzola Green Salad

Kenny Phillips, *Jacksonville, FL*

Antipasto Kabobs

Easy-to-pick-up party food! Add some crunchy bread sticks for a light meal.

Makes 16 servings

⅓ c. olive oil
⅓ c. balsamic vinegar
1 T. fresh thyme, minced
1 clove garlic, minced
1 t. sugar
9-oz. pkg. cheese-filled tortellini, cooked
5-oz. pkg. thinly sliced salami
12-oz. jar artichoke hearts, drained and
    quartered
5¾-oz. jar green olives with pimentos, drained
16-oz. jar banana peppers, drained
1 pt. cherry tomatoes
16 6-inch skewers, soaked in water

Combine oil, vinegar, thyme, garlic and sugar; set aside. Thread remaining ingredients onto skewers alternately in order given. Arrange skewers in a single layer in a glass or plastic container; drizzle with marinade. Cover and refrigerate for 2 to 3 hours, turning occasionally. Drain and discard marinade before serving.

Debbie Muer, *Encino, CA*

Potato Latkes

This is one of our favorite recipes to serve during Hanukkah. We make them as a family and look forward to celebrating together. The kids love them with applesauce and the adults seem to prefer the sour cream. No matter what you choose, these are delicious!

Serves 4 to 6

2 c. potatoes, peeled and grated
2 eggs, beaten
⅛ t. baking powder
1½ t. salt
1 T. all-purpose flour or matzo meal
⅛ t. pepper
oil for frying
Garnish: sour cream or applesauce

Mix all ingredients except oil and garnish together. Heat oil in a skillet over medium-high heat. Pour about one tablespoon of batter for each pancake into hot oil and fry until golden. Top with a dollop of sour cream or applesauce.

Potato Latkes

Jo Ann, *Gooseberry Patch*

White Christmas Coconut Sheet Cake

Enjoy this sheet cake slathered with lemon curd, whipped cream and plenty of coconut.

Serves 15

18¼-oz. pkg. white cake mix
¾ c. cream of coconut
¼ c. butter, melted
3 eggs
½ c. water
¾ c. lemon curd
4 oz. white melting chocolate, chopped
½ c. sour cream
1 c. whipping cream
¼ c. powdered sugar
6-oz. pkg. frozen grated coconut, thawed
Optional: maraschino cherries with stems,
   lemon zest

Combine first 5 ingredients in a large bowl; beat at low speed with an electric mixer one minute. Increase speed to medium and beat 1½ minutes. Spread batter into a greased and floured 13"x9" baking pan. Bake at 350 degrees for 35 minutes or until a toothpick inserted in center comes out clean. Remove pan to a wire rack; spread lemon curd over hot cake. Let cool completely in pan on wire rack. (Cake will sink slightly in center.) Microwave white chocolate in a small microwave-safe bowl on high one minute or until melted, stirring after 30 seconds. Stir in sour cream. Cover and chill 30 minutes. Beat whipping cream and powdered sugar in a large bowl at medium speed until stiff peaks form. Add white chocolate mixture and beat at low speed just until combined. Spread whipped cream topping over cake; sprinkle with coconut. Cover and chill 8 hours. Garnish with maraschino cherries and lemon zest, if desired. Store in refrigerator.

Christi Ross, *Grundy Center, IA*

Peppermint Punch

My husband's grandmother's recipe. A former restaurant owner, Grandma Ross was known far and wide for this festive and tasty punch.

Serves 8 to 10

1 qt. peppermint ice cream, softened
1 c. milk
2-ltr. bottle ginger ale, chilled
Garnish: peppermint sticks, finely crushed
   or whole

In a large punch bowl, blend together ice cream and milk; stir gently. Slowly add ginger ale; stir until combined. Moisten rims of glasses with water and dip into finely crushed candy. Serve with peppermint stick stirrers, if desired.

Peppermint Punch

Angela Murphy, *Tempe, AZ*

Christmas Breakfast Stratas

These casseroles can be partially made ahead and assembled just before baking. Cook the sausage a day ahead and store in a plastic zipping bag in the refrigerator. The bread can also be cubed a day ahead and stored at room temperature in a plastic zipping bag. These casseroles can also be made in two 11"x7" baking pans.

Serves 20

2 1-lb. pkgs. hot ground pork sausage
16-oz. loaf sliced French bread, cut into 1-inch cubes
4 c. shredded Cheddar and Monterey Jack cheese blend, divided
8-oz. pkg. sliced mushrooms, coarsely chopped
4½-oz. can diced green chiles, drained
4-oz. can sliced ripe olives, drained
8 eggs, lightly beaten
4 c. milk
1 t. salt
1 t. onion powder
1 t. dry mustard
1 t. dried oregano
¼ t. pepper
Optional: sour cream, salsa

Cook the sausage in a large skillet over medium-high heat, stirring until it crumbles and is no longer pink. Drain and set aside. Divide the bread cubes between a lightly greased 13"x9" baking pan and an 8"x8" baking pan. Divide 2 cups cheese over bread cubes. Sprinkle with cooked sausage, mushrooms, green chiles and olives. Whisk together the eggs and the next 6 ingredients in a medium bowl. Pour mixture over casseroles. Sprinkle with remaining cheese. Bake, uncovered, at 350 degrees for one hour or until set. Garnish with sour cream and salsa, if desired.

> **⟨ Christmas Casual ⟩**
>
> Start off Christmas Day with some family fun! Get the family involved in making biscuits from scratch. Start a bowl of fruit salad the night before and do the prep work for Christmas Breakfast Stratas. While the biscuits bake, let the coffee perk and the children peek in their stockings.

Christmas Breakfast Stratas

Michelle Case, *Yardley, PA*

Break-of-Day Berry Parfait

So pretty served in a parfait or champagne glass on Christmas morning.

Serves 2

1 c. strawberries, hulled and sliced
½ c. raspberries
¼ c. blackberries
1 c. bran & raisin cereal
6-oz. container strawberry yogurt

In a bowl, combine berries; divide into 2 small bowls. Top each with cereal. Spoon the yogurt over the top.

Jennie Gist, *Gooseberry Patch*

Pineapple Wassail

Bring to a holiday open house while warm... mmmm!

Makes about 2 quarts

4 c. unsweetened pineapple juice
12-oz. can apricot nectar
2 c. apple cider
1½ c. orange juice
2 3-inch cinnamon sticks
1 t. whole cloves
4 cardamom seeds, crushed

Combine all ingredients in a 3-quart slow cooker. Reduce heat and simmer 15 to 20 minutes; strain into serving glasses or punchbowl. Serve warm.

Jill Ball, *Highland, UT*

Sweet Apple Tarts

I like to use Granny Smith apples in these tarts, but you can use any good baking apple that you like. Everyone loves it for our Christmas dessert.

Serves 9

1 sheet frozen puff pastry, thawed
½ c. apricot jam
4 Granny Smith apples, peeled, cored and very
   thinly sliced
¼ c. brown sugar, packed
½ t. cinnamon
½ c. pistachio nuts, chopped
Optional: vanilla ice cream

Roll pastry into a 12-inch square on a lightly floured surface. Cut pastry into nine 3-inch squares. Arrange squares on an ungreased baking sheet; pierce with a fork. Spoon jam evenly over each square; arrange apple slices over jam. Combine brown sugar and cinnamon in a small bowl; mix well. Sprinkle over apple slices. Bake at 400 degrees for 20 to 25 minutes, until pastry is golden and apples are crisp-tender. Sprinkle with nuts. Serve warm topped with scoops of ice cream, if desired.

Sweet Apple Tarts

Cherylann Smith, *Efland, NC*

Herbed Sausage Quiche

Serve this quiche right from the table...it is so pretty to serve on Christmas morning.

Makes 8 servings

9-inch frozen pie crust, thawed
1 c. ground pork breakfast sausage, browned
    and drained
3 eggs, beaten
1 c. 2 % milk
1 c. shredded Cheddar cheese
1 sprig fresh rosemary, chopped
1½ t. Italian seasoning
¼ t. salt
¼ t. pepper

Bake pie crust according to package directions. Mix together remaining ingredients in a bowl; spread into baked crust. Bake, uncovered, at 450 degrees for 15 minutes. Reduce oven temperature to 350 degrees, cover with foil and bake 9 more minutes. Cut into wedges to serve.

Joyce LaMure, *Sequim, WA*

Cranberry-Orange Scones

I received this recipe from a friend a few years ago. They're not only yummy, but quick & easy to make.

Serves 10

2 c. biscuit baking mix
½ c. sugar
½ c. butter, softened
1 egg, beaten
½ c. dried cranberries
½ c. chopped pecans
1 T. orange zest
2½ to 3 T. buttermilk
Garnish: beaten egg white, sanding sugar

Combine baking mix, sugar and butter until crumbly. Make a well in the center and add egg; stir to blend. Stir in cranberries, pecans and zest. Add buttermilk as needed for dough to form a soft ball. Place dough on lightly floured surface and knead 3 or 4 times. Flatten dough and shape into an 8-inch circle. Using a serrated knife, cut dough in triangles. Brush with egg white and garnish with sugar. Arrange on a lightly oiled baking sheet and bake at 400 degrees for 10 to 15 minutes, or until golden.

Cranberry-Orange Scones

Barbara McCurry, *Carpinteria, CA*

Barbara's Open-House Waffles

Every Saturday morning, I serve these for family & friends...it's fun, and the neighbors love it!

Serves 6 to 8

3 c. biscuit baking mix
1 c. millet flour
⅛ t. baking soda
¼ c. canola oil
3 eggs, beaten
3 c. buttermilk
2 T. water
Garnish: maple syrup, fresh strawberries, whipped cream

In a bowl, whisk together baking mix, flour and baking soda. Add remaining ingredients except garnish and mix well. Drop batter by ½ cupfuls onto a heated waffle iron; cook according to manufacturer's directions. Top with maple syrup, strawberries and whipped cream.

Angela Leikem, *Silverton, OR*

Christmas Morning Chile Relleno

Serve with fruit salad and sausage links for a spicy Christmas breakfast.

Serves 8 to 10

6-oz. pkg. shredded Cheddar cheese
16-oz. pkg. shredded Monterey Jack cheese
2 4-oz. cans chopped green chiles
4 eggs
1 c. evaporated milk
¼ c. all-purpose flour
Garnish: cherry tomatoes, fresh parsley

Sprinkle cheeses and chiles together alternately in a greased 13"x9" baking pan. Whisk together eggs, milk and flour in a medium bowl and pour over cheese mixture. Bake, uncovered, at 350 degrees for 30 minutes. Let cool slightly before serving.

⤳ Presentation ⤲

Many of your favorite recipes can be dressed up for the holidays with just a little red and green garnish. Use cut tomatoes, fresh herbs, fresh red pepper and other red and green garnishes that suit the recipe.

Christmas Morning Chile Relleno

Jo Ann, *Gooseberry Patch*

Easy Fancy Broccoli

Bagged broccoli flowerets make this side dish a cinch to prepare!

Serves 6

1/3 c. pine nuts
1/4 c. butter
1 T. olive oil
6 cloves garlic, thinly sliced
1 lb. broccoli flowerets
1/2 t. salt
1/8 t. red pepper flakes

Toast pine nuts in a large skillet over medium heat 6 minutes or until lightly browned. Remove from skillet and set aside. Heat butter and oil in same skillet over medium heat until butter melts. Add garlic; sauté one to 2 minutes or until lightly browned. Add broccoli, salt and red pepper flakes. Sauté 8 minutes or until broccoli is tender. Stir in pine nuts before serving.

Vickie, *Gooseberry Patch*

Rosemary Pork & Mushrooms

This simple dish is delicious with ordinary button mushrooms, but for a special dinner I'll use a combination of wild mushrooms... their earthy flavor goes so well with the fresh rosemary.

Makes 4 servings, 2 slices each

1 lb. pork tenderloin, cut into 8 slices
1 T. butter
1 c. sliced mushrooms
2 T. onion, finely chopped
1 clove garlic, minced
1 t. fresh rosemary, chopped
1/4 t. celery salt
1 T. sherry or apple juice

Flatten each pork slice to one-inch thick; set aside. Melt butter in a large skillet over medium-high heat. Cook pork slices just until golden, about one minute per side. Remove pork slices to a plate, reserving drippings in skillet. Add remaining ingredients except sherry or apple juice to skillet. Reduce heat to low; cook for 2 minutes, stirring frequently. Stir in sherry or juice. Return pork slices to skillet; spoon mushroom mixture over top. Cover and simmer for 3 to 4 minutes, until the pork juices run clear. Serve pork slices topped with mushroom mixture.

Rosemary Pork & Mushrooms

Sandy Bogan, *Waldorf, MD*

Eggnog French Toast Strata

A convenient overnight make-ahead for breakfast.

Makes 6 to 8

1 loaf French bread, sliced
3-oz. pkg. cream cheese, softened
2½ c. eggnog
6 T. butter, melted
8 eggs, beaten
¼ t. nutmeg

Arrange enough bread slices to cover the bottom of a greased 13"x9" baking pan. Spread cream cheese over bread; arrange remaining bread over top. Whisk together eggnog, butter and eggs until blended. Pour evenly over bread. With back of spoon, gently press bread into dish. Sprinkle with nutmeg. Cover and refrigerate for 8 hours to overnight. Uncover; bake at 325 degrees for 30 to 35 minutes, until center is set and edges are golden. Let stand for 10 minutes; cut into squares. Serve with warm Cranberry Syrup. servings.

CRANBERRY SYRUP:

1 c. frozen raspberry juice concentrate, thawed
1 c. whole-berry cranberry sauce
⅓ c. sugar

Combine in a saucepan over low heat. Cook and whisk until bubbly.

Lillian Dahlstrom, *Ames, IA*

Festive Cranberry Honey

This recipe makes enough to give several gifts. Save jelly and jam jars to use to hold your homemade variety. To make a pretty topper, cut holly-shaped leaves from scrapbook paper and adhere to the top of the jar. Thread some red wood beads to serve as little berries.

Makes about 8 cups

3 16-oz. cans whole-berry cranberry sauce
12-oz. jar orange marmalade
1½ c. honey

Place cranberry sauce and marmalade in a large microwave-safe bowl. Microwave on high 2 minutes or until melted. Stir in honey until well blended. Spoon into jars with lids. Store in the refrigerator. Serve with breads or use as a glaze for meat.

Festive Cranberry Honey

Robin Cornett, *Spring Hill, FL*

Cape Cod Clam Chowder

For smoky flavor, stir in some crisply cooked and crumbled bacon.

Serves 6 to 8

2 10¾-oz. cans New England clam chowder
10¾-oz. can cream of celery soup
10¾-oz. can cream of potato soup
2 pts. half-and-half
3 potatoes, peeled and diced
salt and pepper to taste
Optional: chopped fresh chives

Combine soups and half-and-half in a large stockpot. Place over medium-low heat until heated through, stirring often. Set aside over low heat. Boil potatoes in water for about 10 minutes; drain and add to soup mixture. Cook over medium heat until potatoes are tender. Add salt and pepper to taste. Garnish with chives, if desired.

Christian Brown, *Killeen, TX*

Deep South Chicken & Dumplings

This delicious comfort food is our family favorite. We love it on Christmas Eve right before we open presents!

Serves 8

4-lb. roasting chicken
salt and pepper to taste
Garnish: fresh parsley

Bake chicken, covered, in an ungreased roasting pan at 350 degrees for 1½ hours. Let chicken cool while preparing Supreme Sauce. Shred chicken; add to simmering sauce in Dutch oven. Drop Dumplings into sauce by heaping tablespoonfuls. Cover and cook over high heat 10 to 15 minutes, until dumplings are firm and puffy. Discard bay leaves. Add salt and pepper; garnish with fresh parsley.

SUPREME SAUCE:

2 T. butter
1 T. oil
½ c. carrot, peeled and diced
½ c. celery, diced
3 cloves garlic, minced
2 bay leaves
5 T. all-purpose flour
6 c. low-sodium chicken broth
¼ c. 2% milk

Melt butter and oil in a Dutch oven over medium heat. Add vegetables, garlic and bay leaves. Sauté until soft. Stir in flour; add broth, one cup at a time, stirring well after each addition. Simmer until thickened; stir in milk.

DUMPLINGS:

2 c. all-purpose flour
1 T. baking powder
1 t. salt
2 eggs
¾ to 1 c. buttermilk, divided

Mix flour, baking powder and salt. Whisk together eggs and ¾ cup buttermilk; fold into flour mixture. Stir just until dough forms, adding a little more buttermilk if needed.

Deep South Chicken & Dumplings

Jessica Heimbaugh, *Gilbert, IA*

Christmas Eve Soup

My mom and I wanted to share one of our favorite recipes. We always have this soup on Christmas Eve...we hope you'll enjoy it too!

Serves 8

2 c. potatoes, peeled and diced
½ c. carrot, peeled and diced
½ c. celery, chopped
¼ c. onion, chopped
2 c. water
1½ t. salt
¼ t. pepper
1 c. cooked ham, cubed
¼ c. butter
¼ c. all-purpose flour
2 c. milk
8-oz. pkg. shredded Cheddar cheese

Combine vegetables, water, salt and pepper in a large soup pot. Bring to a boil over medium heat. Reduce heat; cover and simmer until vegetables are tender. Stir in ham; set aside. In a separate saucepan, melt butter; stir in flour until smooth. Gradually add milk; bring to a boil. Cook and stir for 2 minutes, until thickened. Stir in cheese until melted; add to vegetable mixture and heat through.

Jen Sell, *Farmington, MN*

Chicken Cordon Bleu

A special dish I serve family & friends during holiday time. It is delicious and beautiful every time.

Makes 4 servings

4 4-oz. boneless, skinless chicken breasts
2 slices deli ham, cut in half
2 slices Swiss cheese, cut in half
1 egg, beaten
½ c. skim milk
¼ c. whole-grain bread crumbs
½ t. garlic powder
1 t. dried oregano
2 T. grated Parmesan cheese

Flatten chicken breasts between 2 pieces of wax paper until ¼-inch thick. Top each piece with a ½ slice of ham and cheese; roll up tightly, securing with toothpicks. In a small bowl, beat egg and milk together; set aside. In another bowl, combine bread crumbs, garlic powder, oregano and Parmesan cheese. Dip each chicken bundle in egg mixture, then in bread crumbs. Place on a greased baking sheet; bake at 350 degrees for 45 minutes.

Chicken Cordon Bleu

Linda Karner, *Pisgah Forest, NC*

Shrimp Scampi & Asparagus

This special dish is a family favorite at the holidays or anytime.

Makes 6 servings

16-oz. pkg. linguine pasta, uncooked
1 T. salt
2 T. butter
2 T. olive oil
1 lb. asparagus, trimmed and cut into bite-size
    pieces
2 cloves garlic, minced
2 lbs. medium shrimp, peeled and cleaned
2 T. mixed fresh herbs like basil, thyme,
    oregano and chives, chopped
2 T. capers, drained
juice of ½ lemon
salt and pepper to taste
Garnish: shredded Parmesan cheese

Cook pasta according to package directions, adding salt to cooking water; drain when pasta is just tender. Meanwhile, in a large skillet over medium heat, melt butter with olive oil. Add asparagus and sauté until partially tender, about 5 minutes. Stir in garlic and shrimp. Cook until shrimp is bright pink, about 5 to 7 minutes. Add herbs, capers and lemon juice; heat through. Season with salt and pepper. Add pasta to mixture in skillet; toss well. If desired, sprinkle with Parmesan cheese.

Wendy Lee Paffenroth, *Pine Island, NY*

Mom's Beef Stroganoff

So rich and creamy, I love to serve it on Christmas Eve. It is always a hit!

Serves 4

½ c. all-purpose flour
1 t. paprika
1 t. dry mustard
1 t. salt
½ t. pepper
1½ lbs. stew beef, sliced into strips
2 T. olive oil
1 onion, thinly sliced
¾ lb. sliced mushrooms
1 c. water
14½-oz. can beef broth
½ c. sour cream
8-oz. pkg. wide egg noodles, cooked
Garnish: paprika, dried parsley

Combine flour and seasonings in a large plastic zipping bag. Add beef; seal and shake until all the meat is coated. Remove meat; reserve flour in plastic zipping bag. Heat oil in a Dutch oven over medium heat; brown meat on all sides. Add onion and mushrooms; sauté. Sprinkle with reserved flour; stir to mix. Add water and broth; stir. Reduce heat; cook for about one hour, until sauce is thickened and meat is tender. Remove from heat; stir in sour cream. Do not boil. Place noodles in large serving dish; spoon meat mixture over noodles. Sprinkle with paprika and parsley if desired.

Mom's Beef Stroganoff

Jen Licon-Connor, *Gooseberry Patch*

Market-Fresh Carrots

A zippy side dish...ready in only 10 minutes! Yes, it is easy, but it is oh-so-good!

Serves 4

1 T. olive oil
3 c. baby carrots
1½ T. balsamic vinegar
1 T. brown sugar, packed

Heat oil in a skillet over medium heat. Add carrots; sauté for 10 minutes, or until tender. Stir in vinegar and brown sugar; toss to coat.

Gina McClenning, *Valrico, FL*

Tuscan Pork Loin

Our holiday guests always ask for this recipe. It makes a lot, but leftovers are delicious the next day. Instead of using plain cream cheese, try garlic-and-herb spreadable cheese.

Serves 10

4-lb. boneless pork tenderloin roast
8-oz. pkg. light cream cheese, softened
1 T. dried pesto seasoning
½ c. baby spinach
4 slices bacon, crisply cooked
12-oz. jar roasted red peppers, drained and divided
1 t. paprika
½ t. salt
½ t. pepper
Optional: additional baby spinach

Slice pork lengthwise, cutting down center, but not through other side. Open halves and cut down center of each half, cutting to, but not through other sides. Open pork into a rectangle. Place pork between 2 sheets of heavy-duty plastic wrap and flatten into an even thickness using a rolling pin or the flat side of a meat mallet. Spread cream cheese evenly over pork. Sprinkle with pesto seasoning; arrange spinach over cream cheese. Top with bacon slices and half of red peppers; reserve remaining red peppers for another recipe. Roll up pork lengthwise; tie at 2-inch intervals with kitchen string. Rub pork with paprika, salt and pepper. Place roast seam-side down on a lightly greased rack on an aluminum foil-lined baking sheet. Bake at 425 degrees for 30 minutes, or until a meat thermometer inserted into thickest portion registers 145 degrees. Remove from oven; let stand for 10 minutes. Remove string from pork; slice pork into ½-inch thick servings. Serve pork slices on a bed of spinach leaves, if desired.

Tuscan Pork Loin

Vickie, *Gooseberry Patch*

Citrus Mimosa

Makes the champagne go a little further! If you prefer, substitute carbonated water for the champagne.

Serves 8

1 c. prepared strawberry daiquiri mix
¾ c. cold water
6-oz. can frozen orange juice concentrate, thawed
¾ c. fresh grapefruit juice
⅓ c. frozen lemonade concentrate, thawed
3 T. frozen limeade concentrate, thawed
1 bottle champagne, chilled
Optional: orange zest curls

Combine prepared daiquiri mix, water, orange juice concentrate, grapefruit juice, lemonade and limeade concentrates in a pitcher or bowl. Stir until well combined. Cover and chill. To serve, pour an equal amount of the chilled mixture and champagne into each glass. Garnish with orange zest curls, if desired.

Jo Ann, *Gooseberry Patch*

Jo Ann's Holiday Brie

One of my favorite holiday recipes...great for "pop-in" guests because it's so quick & easy to prepare.

Serves 6 to 8

13.2-oz. pkg. Brie cheese
¼ c. caramel ice cream topping
½ c. sweetened dried cranberries
½ c. dried apricots, chopped
½ c. chopped pecans
assorted crackers

Place Brie on an ungreased microwave-safe dish; microwave, uncovered, on high 10 to 15 seconds. Cut out a wedge to see if center is soft. If center is still firm, microwave cheese an additional 5 to 10 seconds, until cheese is soft and spreadable. Watch carefully, as the center will begin to melt quickly. Drizzle with caramel topping; sprinkle with cranberries, apricots and nuts. Serve with crackers.

Jo Ann's Holiday Brie

Angela Murphy, *Tempe, AZ*

Tomato Cocktail

A great appetizer to serve while you're putting the finishing touches on brunch.

Serves 6

46-oz. can of tomato juice
juice of ½ a lemon
1 t. sweet onion, grated
1 t. Worcestershire sauce
⅛ t. hot pepper sauce
celery sticks for garnish

Combine all ingredients except celery sticks; chill. Garnish with celery sticks.

Marcy Richardson, *Robbinsdale, MN*

Salted Nut Squares

These little gems are just like eating a candy bar. They are so easy to make and everyone just loves them!

Makes 2 dozen

16-oz. jar dry-roasted peanuts, divided
¼ c. butter
10-oz. pkg. peanut butter chips
14-oz. can sweetened condensed milk
10½-oz. pkg. marshmallows

Spread half of peanuts in a lightly greased 13"x9" baking pan. Combine butter, peanut butter chips and condensed milk in a saucepan over medium heat; stir until melted and well blended. Stir in marshmallows until melted; spread marshmallow mixture over peanuts. Sprinkle remaining peanuts over top; gently press down into marshmallow mixture. Cool; chill until set, about one hour. Slice into squares.

Mary Ary, *Lexington, KY*

English Cider

This warm and spicy drink is yummy any time of year, but especially when winter is in the air! I love to serve this after we go Christmas caroling in our neighborhood.

Makes 6 to 8 servings

½ c. brown sugar, packed
1½ qts. apple cider
1 t. whole allspice
2 cinnamon sticks
2 t. whole cloves
1 orange, sliced and seeded

Combine ingredients in a large stockpot. Spices can be placed in a tea strainer, if preferred, or added loose. Cover and simmer for 25 minutes. Strain before serving if necessary.

English Cider

Jeanne West, *Roanoke Rapids, NC*

Easy Slow-Cooker Potato Soup

When it is cold outside, everyone loves to come home to a bowl of this yummy soup.

Serves 4 to 6

4 to 5 potatoes, peeled and cubed
10¾-oz. can cream of celery soup
10¾-oz. can cream of chicken soup
1⅓ c. water
4⅔ c. milk
6.6-oz. pkg. instant mashed potato flakes
Optional: bacon bits, green onions, shredded
   Cheddar cheese

Place potatoes, soups and water in a 5-quart slow cooker. Cover and cook on high setting 2 to 3 hours or until potatoes are tender. Add milk and instant mashed potato flakes to reach desired consistency, stirring constantly. Cover and cook 2 to 3 hours longer; spoon into bowls to serve. Top with bacon bits, green onions and Cheddar cheese, if desired.

Dawn Hedding, *Bowling Green, OH*

Hoppin' John

This dish is popular in the South. It's traditionally eaten on New Year's Day and promises good luck.

Serves 4 to 6

1 c. dried black-eyed peas
10 c. water, divided
6 slices bacon, coarsely chopped
¾ c. onion, chopped
1 stalk celery, chopped
¾ t. cayenne pepper
1½ t. salt
1 c. long-cooking rice, uncooked

Rinse peas and place in a large saucepan with 6 cups water. Bring to a boil; reduce heat and simmer 2 minutes. Remove from heat, cover and let stand one hour. Drain and rinse. In same pan, cook bacon until crisp, reserving 3 tablespoons drippings in pan. Add peas, remaining water, onion, celery, cayenne pepper and salt. Bring to a boil, cover and reduce heat. Simmer 30 minutes. Add rice; cover and simmer 20 more minutes or until peas and rice are tender.

Hoppin' John

Lisa Langston, *Conroe, TX*

Black-Eyed Pea Caviar

This is a favorite holiday dip that we always serve on New Year's Eve. It is delicious with any kind of chips.

Makes 4¹/₂ cups

2 15-oz. cans black-eyed peas, drained
1 yellow or green pepper, finely chopped
¹/₂ c. roasted red peppers packed in oil, drained and finely chopped
¹/₂ c. red onion, minced
¹/₂ c. fresh cilantro or parsley, minced
¹/₄ c. olive oil
2 cloves garlic, minced
2 T. white wine vinegar
1 t. ground cumin
2 t. coarse-grain mustard
¹/₄ t. salt
pita chips

Combine all ingredients in a medium-size bowl except pita chips; stir well. Cover and chill several hours. Serve at room temperature with pita chips.

Elizabeth Burkhalter, *Oshkosh, WI*

Champagne Fruit Salad

This delicious recipe is really more of a dessert than a salad. We love it no matter what you call it. We serve it on New Year's Eve in pretty glasses.

Serves 12

8-oz. pkg. cream cheese, softened
³/₄ c. sugar
10-oz. pkg. frozen sliced strawberries, thawed and drained
2 bananas, sliced
8-oz. can crushed pineapple, drained
1 c. chopped pecans
1 c. sweetened flaked coconut
10-oz. container frozen whipped topping, thawed

In a large bowl, blend together cream cheese and sugar with an electric mixer on medium speed. Stir in remaining ingredients by hand. Spread in a 3-quart baking pan. Cover and freeze until firm, 3 to 4 hours. Remove from freezer a few minutes before serving time; cut into squares. Serve in champagne glasses, if desired.

Champagne Fruit Salad

Sue Bodner, *New York, NY*

Jalapeño Poppers

At holiday time we often have guest over for appetizers. Everyone brings their favorite appetizer. This one seems to disappear very quickly!

Makes 2 dozen

24 pickled jalapeño peppers
1 lb. Cheddar cheese
½ c. cornmeal
½ c. all-purpose flour
1 t. salt
2 eggs, beaten
oil for deep frying

Make a short slit into each jalapeño pepper; remove as many seeds as possible. Slice cheese into strips ¼-inch wide and one-inch long; insert one in each jalapeño. Combine cornmeal, flour and salt in a small bowl; place beaten eggs in a separate bowl. Dip peppers into egg mixture; roll in cornmeal mixture until well coated. Set aside on a wire rack for 30 minutes. Add 4 inches of oil to a deep fryer; heat to about 375 degrees. Add poppers in small batches; cook until crisp and golden, about 4 minutes. Remove poppers using a slotted spoon; drain on paper towels.

Jo Ann, *Gooseberry Patch*

Party Paella Casserole

Here's a great use for rotisserie chicken, shrimp and yellow rice. We like to serve this on New Year's Eve or at our Super Bowl party.

Serves 8

2 8-oz. pkgs. yellow rice, uncooked
1 lb. medium shrimp, cleaned
1 T. fresh lemon juice
½ t. salt
¼ t. pepper
2 cloves garlic, minced
1½ T. olive oil
2½-lb. lemon-and-garlic deli-roasted whole
    chicken, coarsely shredded
5 green onions, chopped
8-oz. container sour cream
1 c. frozen English peas, thawed
1 c. green olives with pimentos, coarsely
    chopped
1½ c. shredded Monterey Jack cheese
½ t. smoked Spanish paprika

Prepare rice according to package directions. Remove from heat and let cool 30 minutes; fluff with a fork. Meanwhile, toss shrimp with lemon juice, salt and pepper in a bowl. Sauté seasoned shrimp and garlic in hot oil in a large non-stick skillet 2 minutes or just until done. Remove from heat. Combine shredded chicken, rice, green onions, sour cream and peas in a large bowl; toss well. Add shrimp and olives, tossing gently. Spoon rice mixture into a greased 13"x9" baking pan. Combine cheese and paprika, tossing well; sprinkle over casserole. Bake, uncovered, at 400 degrees for 15 minutes or just until cheese is melted and casserole is thoroughly heated.

Party Paella Casserole

Carol Hickman, *Kingsport, TN*

Cheese Pops

These are fun to eat and to make.
Always a hit!

Makes 3 to 4 dozen

2 3-oz. pkgs. cream cheese, softened
2 c. finely shredded Cheddar cheese
2 t. honey
1½ c. carrots, peeled and finely shredded
1 c. pecans, finely chopped
4 doz. pretzel sticks

Combine cheeses, honey and carrots; chill for
one hour. Shape into one-inch balls and then roll
in pecans. Chill, then insert pretzel sticks before
serving.

Beth Kramer, *Port St. Lucie, FL*

Orange Coffee Rolls

Perfect for Christmas morning, these rolls are
our family favorite.

Makes 2 dozen

1 env. active dry yeast
¼ c. warm water, 110 to 115 degrees
1 c. sugar, divided
2 eggs
½ c. sour cream
¼ c. plus 2 T. butter, melted
1 t. salt
2¾ to 3 c. all-purpose flour
2 T. butter, melted and divided
1 c. flaked coconut, toasted and divided
2 T. orange zest

Combine the yeast and the warm water
in a large bowl; let stand 5 minutes. Add ¼ cup
sugar and next 4 ingredients; beat at medium
speed with an electric mixer until blended.
Gradually stir in enough flour to make a soft
dough. Turn dough out onto a well-floured
surface; knead until smooth and elastic (about
5 minutes). Place in a well greased bowl, turning
to grease top. Cover and let rise in a warm place
(85 degrees), free from drafts, 1½ hours or until
double in bulk. Punch dough down and divide
in half. Roll one portion of dough into a 12-inch
circle; brush with one tablespoon melted butter.
Combine remaining sugar, ¾ cup coconut and
orange zest; sprinkle half of coconut mixture
over dough. Cut into 12 wedges; roll up each
wedge, beginning at wide end. Place in a greased
13"x9" baking pan, point-side down. Repeat with
remaining dough, butter and coconut mixture.
Cover and let rise in a warm place, free from
drafts, 45 minutes or until double in bulk. Bake at
350 degrees for 25 to 30 minutes or until golden.
(Cover with aluminum foil after 15 minutes to
prevent excessive browning, if necessary.) Spoon
warm Glaze over warm rolls; sprinkle with
remaining coconut.

GLAZE:

¾ c. sugar
½ c. sour cream
¼ c. butter
2 t. orange juice

Combine all ingredients in a small saucepan;
bring to a boil. Boil 3 minutes, stirring
occasionally. Let cool slightly. Makes 1⅛ cups.

Orange Coffee Rolls

Ashlee Haefs, *Buna, TX*

Red Velvet Pancakes

Red velvet cake is one of my family's favorites, so with this recipe we can have it for breakfast...what a great way to start the day! Make them in heart shapes for Valentine's day for the ones you love.

Makes one dozen pancakes

1½ c. all-purpose flour
2 T. baking cocoa
4 t. sugar
1½ t. baking powder
½ t. baking soda
1 t. cinnamon
1 t. salt
2 eggs
1¼ c. buttermilk
1 T. red food coloring
1½ t. vanilla extract
¼ c. butter, melted
Garnish: maple syrup, butter, whipped cream cheese

In a bowl, whisk together all dry ingredients. In a separate bowl, mix eggs, buttermilk, food coloring and vanilla. Add to dry ingredients and mix well. Fold in melted butter. Using an ice cream scoop, drop batter onto a lightly greased, hot griddle and cook until edges darken, about 5 minutes. Flip and cook until done. Serve topped with syrup and butter or whipped cream cheese.

Melonie Klosterho, *Fairbanks, AK*

Easy Cherry Cobbler

This is a fun treat to celebrate Presidents' day in February. Our entire family loves this dessert!

Serves 8

15-oz. can tart red cherries
1 c. all-purpose flour
1 c. sugar, divided
1 c. 2% milk
2 t. baking powder
⅛ t. salt
¼ c. butter, melted
Optional: vanilla ice cream or whipped topping

Bring cherries with juice to a boil in a saucepan over medium heat; remove from heat. Mix flour, ¾ cup sugar, milk, baking powder and salt in a medium bowl. Pour butter into 6 one-cup ramekins or into a 2-quart casserole dish; pour flour mixture over butter. Add cherries; do not stir. Sprinkle remaining sugar over top. Bake at 400 degrees for 20 to 30 minutes. Serve warm with ice cream or whipped cream, if desired.

Easy Cherry Cobbler

Sarah Sommers, *Atwater, CA*

Party Cheese Balls

For a festive presentation, roll up this flavorful mixture into 7 mini cheese balls. For just one, proceed as directed in the recipe, rolling mixture into one large ball.

Makes 7 mini balls or one large ball

2 8-oz. pkgs. cream cheese, softened
2 c. shredded sharp Cheddar cheese
1 t. pimento, chopped
1 t. onion, minced
1 t. lemon juice
1 t. green pepper, chopped
2 t. Worcestershire sauce
$\frac{1}{8}$ t. cayenne pepper
$\frac{1}{8}$ t. salt
Optional: chopped pecans

Blend cream cheese until light and fluffy; add Cheddar cheese and next 7 ingredients. Shape into 7 mini balls; wrap in plastic wrap and refrigerate until firm. Roll in pecans, if desired.

Shay Gardner, *Portland, OR*

Ultimate Cheeseburger Pizza

This pizza is a complete meal. I like to serve it when we watch the Super Bowl game with friends. Everyone loves it!

Serves 4

$\frac{1}{2}$ lb. lean ground beef
$14\frac{1}{2}$-oz. can whole tomatoes, drained and chopped
1 t. garlic, minced
12-inch prebaked pizza crust
$1\frac{1}{2}$ c. shredded Cheddar cheese
$\frac{1}{4}$ c. green onions, chopped
$\frac{1}{2}$ t. salt

Brown beef in a skillet over medium-high heat, stirring often, 4 minutes or until beef crumbles and is no longer pink; drain well. Stir together tomatoes and garlic. Spread crust evenly with tomato mixture; sprinkle with ground beef, cheese, green onions and salt. Bake at 450 degrees directly on oven rack for 12 to 14 minutes or until cheese is melted.

~ **Kitchen Helper** ~

To avoid having to get out the cutting board, use kitchen shears to chop tomatoes while they are still in the can.

Ultimate Cheeseburger Pizza

Sonna Johnson, *Goldfield, IA*

Dipped & Drizzled Pretzels

A pretty and tasty gift. Make these sweet treats for any special holiday event and watch them disappear!

Makes 5 cups

18-oz. pkg. white melting chocolate, divided
4 c. small pretzel twists
pink paste food coloring

Melt 12 ounces white chocolate in a double boiler. Dip pretzels in melted chocolate and place on wax paper to harden. Melt remaining 6 ounces white chocolate in a small saucepan and tint pink; drizzle over pretzels. Allow to harden. Store in an airtight container.

Athena Colegrove, *Big Springs, TX*

2-Kiss Cupcakes

Bake these for your family and you'll be guaranteed not just kisses, but several hugs, too!

Makes 2½ dozen

¾ c. butter, softened
1⅔ c. sugar
3 eggs, beaten
1½ t. vanilla extract
2 c. all-purpose flour
⅔ c. baking cocoa
1¼ t. baking soda
¼ t. baking powder
1 t. salt
1⅓ c. water
60 milk chocolate drops, divided

Beat butter, sugar, eggs and vanilla; set aside. Combine flour, cocoa, baking soda, baking powder and salt; add alternately with water to butter mixture. Fill paper-lined muffin cups half full. Place a chocolate drop in center of each. Bake at 350 degrees for 20 minutes. Let cool. Frost with Chocolate Frosting. Top each with a chocolate drop.

CHOCOLATE FROSTING:

¼ c. butter, melted
½ c. baking cocoa
⅓ c. milk
1 t. vanilla extract
3½ c. powdered sugar

Combine all ingredients; beat until smooth.

2-Kiss Cupcakes

Marilyn Epley, *Stillwater, OK*

Honeyed Fruit & Rice

Jasmine rice is also known as fragrant rice and can be found in many markets or specialty stores. With the dried fruit added, it makes a lovely holiday dessert.

Makes 2 servings

2 c. cooked jasmine rice
⅓ c. dried cranberries
⅓ c. dried apricots, chopped
¼ c. honey
Garnish: milk

Stir together hot cooked rice, cranberries, apricots and honey. Divide into 2 bowls; top with milk.

> ⌁ **Kitchen Tip** ⌁
>
> There are many kinds of rice at your supermarket. Make a point of looking up what kind of rice works best for each recipe. For example, jasmine rice works well for pudding and Arborio rice for risotto.

Dana Cunningham, *Lafayette, LA*

Be Mine Cherry Brownies

Bake an extra-special Valentine for your sweetie!

Makes 14

18.3-oz. pkg. fudge brownie mix
3 1-oz. sqs. white baking chocolate
⅓ c. whipping cream
1 c. cream cheese frosting
¼ c. maraschino cherries, drained and
    chopped
1½ c. semi-sweet chocolate chips
¼ c. butter
Garnish: candy sprinkles

Prepare brownie mix according to package instructions. Line a 13"x9" baking pan with aluminum foil, leaving several inches on sides for handles. Spray bottom of foil with non-stick vegetable spray; spread batter into pan. Bake at 350 degrees for 24 to 26 minutes; let cool. Lift brownies from pan; remove foil. Use a 3-inch heart-shaped cookie cutter to cut brownies. In a microwave-safe bowl, melt white baking chocolate and whipping cream for one to 2 minutes, stirring until chocolate is melted; refrigerate 30 minutes. Stir frosting and cherries into chilled chocolate mixture; spread over brownies. In a microwave-safe bowl, melt chocolate chips and butter for one to 2 minutes, stirring until smooth. Transfer to a plastic zipping bag, snip off a tip and drizzle over brownies. Garnish with sprinkles.

Be Mine Cherry Brownies

Roger Baker, *La Rue, OH*

Mom's Special-Occasion Cherry Cake

A perfect dessert to enjoy with your sweetheart!

Serves 8 to 10

2¼ c. cake flour
2½ t. baking powder
¼ t. salt
½ c. shortening
1⅓ c. sugar
3 egg whites
⅔ c. milk
10-oz. jar maraschino cherries, drained with
    juice reserved
½ c. chopped walnuts
4-oz. jar maraschino cherries with stems,
    drained

Combine flour, baking powder and salt in a small bowl; set aside. Beat shortening in a large bowl 30 seconds; beat in sugar. Gradually add egg whites, beating well after each addition; set aside. Whisk together milk and ¼ cup reserved cherry juice; add alternately with flour mixture to sugar mixture, mixing well. Fold in nuts and drained cherries; divide batter evenly between 2 lightly greased and floured 8" round cake pans. Bake at 350 degrees for 25 to 30 minutes; cool on a wire rack 10 minutes. Remove from pans to cool completely; spread Butter Frosting between layers and on the top and sides of cake. Decorate top with a ring of stemmed cherries.

BUTTER FROSTING:

¾ c. butter, softened
6 c. powdered sugar, divided
⅓ c. milk
¼ t. salt
1½ t. vanilla extract
4 to 6 drops red food coloring

Beat butter until fluffy; mix in 3 cups powdered sugar. Gradually blend in milk, salt and vanilla; add remaining powdered sugar, mixing well. Stir in food coloring to desired tint.

Kathy Grashoff, *Fort Wayne, IN*

Brie Kisses

I love to make these beautiful appetizers at Christmastime or on Valentine's Day.

Makes 32

⅔ lb. Brie cheese
17.3-oz. pkg. frozen puff pastry
red and/or green hot pepper jelly

Cut Brie into 32 ½-inch cubes; arrange on a plate and place in the freezer. Let pastry thaw at room temperature 30 minutes; unfold each pastry and roll with a rolling pin to remove creases. Slice each sheet into quarters; slice each quarter in half. Cut each piece in half one more time for a total of 32 squares. Place squares into greased mini muffin cups; arrange so corners of dough point upward. Bake at 400 degrees for 5 minutes. Place one Brie cube in center of each pastry. Bake 10 minutes or until edges are golden. Remove from pan. Immediately top with colorful pepper jelly.

Brie Kisses

Shelley Turner, *Boise, ID*

Chocolate Bread

Everyone loves a little chocolate at Valentine time. This bread is sure to please!

Makes 2 loaves

1¼ c. milk
½ c. water
1 env. active dry yeast
4½ c. all-purpose flour, divided
½ c. baking cocoa
¼ c. sugar
1 t. salt
1 egg
2 T. butter, softened
2 4-oz. semi-sweet chocolate bars, chopped
1½ T. turbinado sugar

Heat the milk and the water until warm (110 to 115 degrees). Combine with yeast in a large bowl; whisk until smooth. Let stand 5 minutes. Stir 2 cups flour, cocoa, sugar and salt into yeast mixture; beat at medium speed with an electric mixer until smooth. Beat in egg, butter and 2 cups flour until a soft dough forms. Turn dough out onto a floured surface; knead until smooth (about 6 minutes), adding remaining flour, one tablespoon at a time as needed, to prevent dough from sticking. Fold in chopped chocolate during last minute of kneading. Place dough in a large, lightly greased bowl, turning to coat top. Cover with plastic wrap; let rise in a warm place (85 degrees), free from drafts, one hour and 40 minutes or until double in bulk. Punch down dough. Divide dough in half; gently shape each portion into an 8"x4" oval. Place dough in

2 lightly greased 8½"x4½" loaf pans. Cover and let rise 1½ hours or until double in bulk. Sprinkle loaves with turbinado sugar. Bake at 375 degrees for 25 minutes or until loaves sound hollow when tapped. Remove from pans. Let cool on a wire rack.

Jessica Parker, *Mulvane, KS*

Sweetheart Shakes

Surprise your sweetheart with a frosty and refreshing two-tone shake!

Serves 4

3 c. milk, divided
1 c. vanilla ice cream, softened
3½-oz. pkg. instant vanilla pudding mix, divided
1 c. strawberry ice cream, softened
3 drops red food coloring

Pour 1½ cups milk into a blender; add vanilla ice cream and ⅓ of dry pudding mix. Cover; blend on high until smooth, about 15 seconds. Pour into 4 freezer-safe glasses; freeze for 30 minutes. Combine remaining pudding mix, strawberry ice cream and food coloring in blender; cover and blend until smooth, about 15 seconds. Pour into glasses on top of vanilla portion and serve.

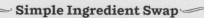

⁓ Simple Ingredient Swap ⁓
Try swapping out ice cream for frozen custard if you're looking for a lighter treat!

Sweetheart Shakes

Melody Taynor, *Everett, WA*

Chocolate-Berry Trifles

I've made all kinds of trifles, but this is my first one with chocolate. My sister says it's my best yet!

Makes 10 servings

1 pt. blueberries, divided
1 pt. strawberries, hulled and sliced
1 angel food cake, cubed
1 c. chocolate syrup
12-oz. container frozen whipped topping, thawed

In a bowl, crush ¼ cup blueberries. Stir in remaining blueberries and strawberries. Place several cake cubes in the bottom of 10 clear serving cups or bowls. Top with a layer of berry mixture. Drizzle lightly with chocolate syrup, then top with a layer of whipped topping. Repeat layers until each cup is full, ending with a layer of whipped topping and a light drizzle of chocolate syrup.

Henry Burnley, *Ankeny, IA*

Brownie Buttons

These little bits of chocolate, caramel and peanut butter will be the sweet goodie they ask for again and again.

Makes 20

16-oz. pkg. refrigerated mini brownie bites dough
11-oz. pkg. assorted mini peanut butter cup candies and chocolate-coated caramels

Spray mini muffin cups with non-stick vegetable spray. Spoon brownie dough evenly into each cup, filling almost full. Bake at 350 degrees for 19 to 20 minutes. Cool in pans 3 to 4 minutes; gently press a candy into each baked brownie until top of candy is level with top of brownie. Cool 10 minutes in pans. Gently twist each brownie to remove from pan. Cool on a wire rack.

⚊ Box of Love ⚊

Tell a best friend no one else can fill her shoes! Cover the lid of a plain shoe box with pictures of shoes cut from magazines or catalogs. Fill the box with homemade treats and wrap the box with pretty cotton string.

Brownie Buttons

Jo Ann, *Gooseberry Patch*

Blueberry-Lemon Crepes

A scrumptious and refreshing breakfast to serve to a special someone!

Makes 6 servings

3-oz. pkg. cream cheese, softened
1½ c. half-and-half
1 T. lemon juice
3¾-oz. pkg. instant lemon pudding mix
½ c. biscuit baking mix
1 egg
6 T. milk
1 c. blueberry pie filling

Combine cream cheese, half-and-half, lemon juice and dry pudding mix in a bowl. Beat with an electric mixer on low speed for 2 minutes. Refrigerate for 30 minutes. Lightly grease a 6" skillet and place over medium-high heat. In a bowl, combine biscuit baking mix, egg and milk. Beat until smooth. Pour 2 tablespoons of batter into skillet for each crepe. Rotating the skillet quickly, allow batter to cover the bottom of the skillet. Cook each crepe until lightly golden, then flip, cooking again until just golden. Spoon 2 tablespoonfuls of cream cheese mixture onto each crepe and roll up. Top with remaining cream cheese mixture and pie filling.

Vickie, *Gooseberry Patch*

Vickie's Chocolate Fondue

Delicious dipping for squares of pound cake, mandarin oranges, cherries and strawberries! This makes a great activity for a Valentine party.

Makes 2½ cups

24-oz. pkg. semi-sweet chocolate chips
1 pt. whipping cream
6 T. corn syrup
6 T. orange extract

Melt chocolate chips in the top of a double boiler; add remaining ingredients and stir to blend. When fondue is warm, spoon into a fondue pot or small slow cooker on low heat to keep sauce warm.

⟨ Presentation ⟩

To make the experience even more special, cut the cake into little heart shapes to dip into the warm chocolate.

Vickie's Chocolate Fondue

Christy Bonner, *Bessemer, AL*

Easy Brunswick Stew

This is a great soup to make for a winter party. Make preparation a breeze by stopping at your local supermarket deli or favorite barbecue restaurant for shredded pork.

Makes 5 quarts

3 lbs. shredded cooked pork

4 c. water

4 c. frozen diced potatoes

3 $14\frac{1}{2}$-oz. cans diced tomatoes with garlic and onion

$14\frac{1}{2}$-oz. can corn, drained

$14\frac{1}{2}$-oz. can cream-style corn

2 c. frozen lima beans

$\frac{1}{2}$ c. barbecue sauce

1 T. hot pepper sauce

$1\frac{1}{2}$ t. salt

1 t. pepper

Stir together all ingredients in a 6-quart stockpot. Bring stew to a boil; cover, reduce heat and simmer, stirring often, 45 minutes.

Vickie, *Gooseberry Patch*

Cheesy Cut-Out Crackers

Dress up any soup or salad when you serve these cheesy crackers. Make them in any shape you like, or cut them into little squares and skip the cookie cutters!

Makes $1\frac{1}{2}$ to 2 dozen

1 c. all-purpose flour

7 T. butter, softened

7 T. shredded Cheddar cheese

$\frac{1}{2}$ t. dried parsley

1 egg yolk

4 t. whipping cream

salt and cayenne pepper to taste

Mix all ingredients together; let rest for about 30 minutes. Roll dough out to about $\frac{1}{8}$-inch thick. Use small cookie cutters to cut out crackers. Bake on ungreased baking sheets at 400 degrees for 8 to 10 minutes, just until golden. Let cool; remove carefully. Store in an airtight container.

Cheesy Cut-Out Crackers

Jo Ann, *Gooseberry Patch*

Crunchy Biscotti

Afternoon or after dinner, you'll crave these treats with your next cup of coffee. I like to dress up these cookies with a drizzle of white chocolate for special holidays!

Makes about 3 dozen cookies

3⅓ c. all-purpose flour
2½ t. baking powder
½ t. salt
¼ c. oil
1¼ c. sugar
2 eggs, beaten
2 egg whites, beaten
Optional: melted white chocolate

Mix flour, baking powder and salt in a large bowl. In a separate bowl, whisk together remaining ingredients except optional chocolate. Blend flour mixture into egg mixture. Divide dough into 3 portions; knead each portion 5 to 6 times, and shape into a ball. Place dough balls on a parchment paper-lined 17"x11" baking sheet. Shape into 9-inch logs; flatten slightly. Bake at 375 degrees for 25 minutes. Remove from oven; place logs on a cutting board. Using a serrated bread knife, cut ½-inch thick slices on a slight diagonal. Return slices to baking sheet, cut-side up. Bake for an additional 10 minutes at 375 degrees. Turn slices over; continue baking for 5 to 7 minutes. Let cool and drizzle with white chocolate, if desired; store in an airtight container.

Ardith Field, *Goldfield, IA*

Mocha Pecan Mud Pie

Two store-bought ice creams pack lots of flavor into this frozen treat that makes a great holiday dessert.

Serves 8

12 chocolate sandwich cookies, crumbled
3 T. butter, melted
1 egg white, lightly beaten
1¼ c. chopped pecans
¼ c. sugar
1 pt. coffee ice cream, softened
1 pt. chocolate ice cream, softened
12 chocolate sandwich cookies, coarsely
    chopped and divided
Optional: frozen whipped topping, thawed,
    additional cookies and pecans, coarsely
    chopped

Stir together cookie crumbs and butter. Press into a 9" pie plate. Brush with egg white. Bake at 350 degrees for 5 minutes. Cool on a wire rack. Place pecans on a lightly greased baking sheet; sprinkle with sugar. Bake at 350 degrees for 8 to 10 minutes. Cool. Stir together ice creams, one cup coarsely chopped cookies and one cup pecans; spoon into crust. Freeze 10 minutes. Press remaining coarsely chopped cookies and pecans on top. Cover and freeze at least 8 hours. Garnish with whipped topping and additional chopped cookies and pecans, if desired.

Mocha Pecan Mud Pie

Carla Turner, *Salem, OR*

Make-Ahead French Toast

This wonderful make-ahead dish is perfect for brunches. With the prep time being the day before, I'm free to visit with family & friends.

Serves 15

3 T. butter
2 baking apples, peeled, cored and sliced
⅓ c. brown sugar, packed
1 T. dark corn syrup
1 t. cinnamon
8 1-inch thick slices French bread
3 eggs, beaten
1 c. milk
1 t. vanilla extract

Melt butter in a heavy skillet over medium heat. Reduce heat to medium-low; add apples and cook, stirring occasionally, until tender. Stir in brown sugar, corn syrup and cinnamon. Cook and stir until brown sugar dissolves. Pour apple mixture into 2 lightly greased 9" pie plates or one, 13"x9" baking pan. Arrange bread slices in one layer on top of apple mixture; set aside. In a medium bowl, whisk together remaining ingredients; pour over bread slices. Cover with plastic wrap and refrigerate overnight. Remove plastic wrap and bake at 375 degrees for 30 to 35 minutes, or until firm and golden. Cool 5 minutes in pan, then invert onto a serving platter.

Sharon Demers, *Bruce Crossing, MI*

Cherry-Pecan Bread Pudding

This old-fashioned bread pudding recipe is one of our favorites. Serve it in February for George Washington's birthday.

Serves 12

2-lb. loaf French bread, cubed
6 c. 2% milk
½ c. plus 2 T. sugar, divided
6 eggs, beaten
2 t. vanilla extract
½ t. cinnamon
½ c. dried tart cherries
½ c. chopped pecans
¼ c. butter, melted

Spread bread cubes on a baking sheet; let dry overnight. Combine milk and 5 tablespoons sugar in a saucepan over low heat. Heat to 120 degrees on a candy thermometer; remove from heat. Whisk together eggs, vanilla, cinnamon and remaining sugar in a large bowl. Stir in cherries and pecans. Slowly whisk half of milk mixture into egg mixture; add remaining milk mixture. Stir in bread cubes; toss to mix and let stand for 5 minutes. Mix in butter; transfer mixture to a lightly greased 13"x9" baking pan. Bake at 350 degrees for 35 minutes, or until center is firm. Serve warm.

Cherry-Pecan Bread Pudding

Jen Licon-Connor, *Gooseberry Patch*

Minty Candy Canes

Easy spritz dough is dressed up for the holidays with a dip of white chocolate and a sprinkle of peppermint.

Makes 5 dozen

¾ c. butter, softened
½ c. sugar
1 t. baking powder
1 egg, beaten
½ t. peppermint extract
1¾ c. all-purpose flour
6 1-oz. sqs. white baking chocolate
1 T. shortening
⅓ c. peppermint candies, finely crushed

In a large bowl, combine butter, sugar and baking powder. Beat with an electric mixer on medium speed until mixed. Add egg and extract; blend well. Beat in as much flour as possible with mixer; stir in any remaining flour. Pack dough into a cookie press fitted with a ½-inch star plate. Press out dough to form 4-inch sticks on ungreased baking sheets, one inch apart; bend into a candy cane shape. Bake at 375 degrees for 7 to 9 minutes, until edges are firm but not brown. Let cool on a wire rack. Melt white chocolate with shortening in a small heavy saucepan over low heat, stirring frequently. Dip the end of each cane into chocolate, letting any excess drip off. Place on wax paper; sprinkle with crushed candies. Let stand until set.

Janis Parr, *Ontario, Canada*

Can't-Be-Beet Cake

Crisscross this yummy cake with pink and white frosting for a festive dessert.

Makes 12 servings

3 eggs, separated
1 c. corn oil
1½ c. sugar
3 T. hot water
2 c. all-purpose flour
2½ t. baking powder
1 t. salt
1 t. cinnamon
1 t. vanilla extract
1 c. chopped pecans
1 c. beets, peeled and grated
1 c. carrots, peeled and grated

In a deep bowl, beat egg whites with an electric mixer on high speed until stiff peaks form; set aside. In a separate large bowl, combine egg yolks and remaining ingredients. Mix well; fold in egg whites. Pour batter into a greased and floured 12"x8" baking pan. Bake at 350 degrees for 35 minutes, or until a toothpick inserted in the center tests done. Cool. Drizzle with Vanilla Icing before slicing.

VANILLA ICING:

1 T. butter, diced
2 c. powdered sugar
2 t. vanilla extract
2 T. hot water
Optional: food coloring

Mix all ingredients in a bowl until consistency of cream.

Can't-Be-Beet Cake

Chapter Three

Spring Celebrations

Enjoy the freshness of spring by celebrating the holidays with both traditional fare and some new twists on old favorites. Celebrate Easter with a traditional Baked Maple Ham studded with whole cloves. Planning a Mother's Day brunch? Make it elegant yet simple with Asparagus & Mushroom Omelets and Colorful Fruit Soup. You'll be celebrating a favorite fruit of the season when you make a beautiful Strawberry Layer Cake for a special dessert. Delight family & friends with the tasty seasonal dishes you find in this chapter of spring holiday favorites.

Tiffany Classen, *Wichita, KS*

Frosty Orange Juice

Thick, frosty and very refreshing!

Makes 4 servings

6-oz. can frozen orange juice concentrate,
   partially thawed
1 c. milk
1 c. water
1 t. vanilla extract
⅓ c. sugar
12 ice cubes

Process all ingredients together in a blender until frothy. Serve in tall glasses.

Eleanor Dionne, *Beverly, MA*

Blueberry Cornmeal Pancakes

Since we like cornmeal muffins as well as anything with blueberries, it's no surprise that these pancakes became a family favorite.

Makes about 24

 1 c. all-purpose flour
1 c. cornmeal
2 T. baking powder
1 T. sugar
1½ c. orange juice
3 T. canola oil
1 egg, beaten
1 c. blueberries, thawed if frozen
Garnish: fresh blueberries, light maple syrup

In a bowl, mix together flour, cornmeal, baking powder and sugar. Add juice, oil and egg; stir well. Gently fold in blueberries. Heat a lightly greased griddle over medium-high heat. Pour batter onto griddle, making small pancakes. Cook pancakes until bubbles appear around the edges; flip and cook on other side. Garnish as desired.

Blueberry Cornmeal Pancakes

Julie Ann Perkins, *Anderson, IN*

Green Goddess Bacon Salad

I remember when Green Goddess salad was so popular in the 1950s. We are so glad it had made a comeback for a new generation to enjoy. We like to add the chicken for more protein and using a deli chicken makes it so quick & easy to make.

Makes 6 servings

7 eggs, hard-boiled, peeled and sliced
7 to 12 slices bacon, chopped and crisply
  cooked
3 c. deli roast chicken, shredded
6 to 8 c. baby spinach
1 red pepper, chopped
Optional: 1 bunch green onions, sliced
Green Goddess salad dressing to taste

In a large salad bowl, combine eggs, bacon, chicken and vegetables; mix well. Pass salad dressing at the table so guests may add it to taste.

Irene Whatling, *West Des Moines, IA*

Colorful Fruit Soup

This soup is so refreshing! My daughter requests it every spring. Freshly ground black pepper complements the sweet fruit wonderfully. Present it on a green tray for St. Patrick's Day!

Makes 6 servings

1 c. seedless grapes, halved
1 c. blueberries
½ c. strawberries, hulled and diced
½ c. pineapple, peeled and diced
½ c. kiwi, peeled and diced
1 c. unsweetened apple juice
½ c. orange juice
¼ t. pepper

Combine fruit in a large bowl. In a measuring cup, mix juices and pepper; pour over fruit mixture. Stir gently. Cover and refrigerate until serving time.

> ∾ **Presentation** ∾
> Bring out your colorful dishes to present your delicious spring recipes. Mismatched colorful napkins will add a fresh look.

Colorful Fruit Soup

Penny Sherman, *Ava, MO*

Grab & Go Breakfast Cookies

These cookies are perfect for those busy mornings when you have to rush out the door.

Makes 1½ dozen

½ c. butter, softened
½ c. sugar
1 egg, beaten
2 T. frozen orange juice concentrate, thawed
1 T. orange zest
1¼ c. all-purpose flour
1 t. baking powder
½ c. wheat & barley cereal

Blend together butter and sugar in a bowl until light and fluffy. Beat in egg, orange juice and zest; set aside. Combine flour and baking powder in a small bowl; stir into butter mixture until blended. Stir in cereal. Drop by tablespoonfuls, 2 inches apart, on an ungreased baking sheet. Bake at 350 degrees for 10 to 12 minutes, until golden around edges. Cool on a wire rack.

Kelly Gray, *Avon Park, FL*

Breakfast Salad with Poached Eggs

This dish may sound odd, but it is really delicious...quick to make too. I serve it often for brunch, while my son requests it often for dinner. I like to add two poached eggs per salad, but you may prefer just one.

Makes 4 servings

4 slices bacon, halved
2 c. water
2 t. vinegar
8 eggs, divided
8 c. spring lettuce mix
1 c. shredded Cheddar cheese
1 c. sliced mushrooms
1 c. sliced black olives
4 roma tomatoes, quartered

Cook bacon in a skillet over medium heat until crisp; drain. Set aside. In another skillet over medium-high heat, bring water and vinegar to a simmer. Crack 2 eggs into water. Cook for 5 to 7 minutes, to desired doneness. Remove eggs with a slotted spoon; repeat with remaining eggs. Divide lettuce among 4 plates. With a slotted spoon, place 2 eggs atop lettuce on each plate; sprinkle with cheese while still hot Arrange vegetables around eggs; arrange bacon on top. Serve immediately.

Breakfast Salad with Poached Eggs

Sister Toni Spencer, *Watertown, SD*

Sunflower Strawberry Salad

A great chilled salad for a spring lunch...it is great for Easter and Mother's Day buffets too.

Makes 6 servings

2 c. strawberries, hulled and sliced
1 apple, cored and diced
1 c. seedless green grapes, halved
$\frac{1}{2}$ c. celery, thinly sliced
$\frac{1}{4}$ c. raisins
$\frac{1}{2}$ c. strawberry yogurt
2 T. sunflower kernels
Optional: lettuce leaves

In a large bowl, combine fruit, celery and raisins. Stir in yogurt. Cover and chill one hour. Sprinkle with sunflower kernels just before serving. Spoon over lettuce leaves, if desired.

Meri Herbert, *Cheboygan, MI*

Carroty Bran Muffins

These muffins are filled with all kinds of goodness. Your entire family will love them and you'll know they are so good for them!

Makes 16 large muffins

$2\frac{1}{2}$ c. all-purpose flour
$2\frac{1}{2}$ c. bran cereal
$1\frac{1}{2}$ c. sugar
$2\frac{1}{2}$ t. baking soda
1 t. salt
2 c. buttermilk
$\frac{1}{3}$ c. applesauce
2 eggs, beaten
$1\frac{1}{2}$ c. carrots, peeled and shredded
1 green apple, cored and chopped
1 c. sweetened dried cranberries
$\frac{1}{2}$ c. chopped walnuts
$\frac{1}{4}$ c. ground flax seed

Mix all ingredients together in a large bowl. Cover and refrigerate batter for up to 2 days, or bake right away. Fill 16 large, greased muffin cups $\frac{2}{3}$ full. Bake at 375 degrees for 15 to 18 minutes; do not overbake. Muffins will become moister if allowed to stand for awhile.

Carroty Bran Muffins

Tammy Rowe, *Bellevue, OH*

Asian Chicken Salad

For some variety, make lettuce wraps using these same ingredients. Separate the lettuce into large leaves, layer with toppings and drizzle with dressing...wrap and eat!

Makes 4 servings

1 head lettuce, shredded
2 to 3 boneless, skinless chicken breasts,
   cooked and shredded
½ c. snow peas
1 bunch green onions, chopped
2 T. slivered almonds
5-oz. can chow mein noodles
2 T. poppy seed

Combine all ingredients in a large salad bowl. Pour Dressing over top and toss well. Serve immediately.

DRESSING:
¼ c. vinegar
2 T. sugar
½ t. salt
½ t. pepper

Whisk ingredients together until well combined.

Audrey Lett, *Newark, DE*

Asparagus & Mushroom Omelet

A delicious way to savor the first tender asparagus of springtime. Add a sprinkle of shredded cheese, if you like.

Makes 3 servings

½ lb. asparagus, trimmed and cut into 1-inch
   pieces
2 T. butter, divided
½ lb. sliced mushrooms
1 clove garlic, minced
4 eggs, lightly beaten
2 T. skim milk
¾ t. dried basil or thyme
½ t. salt
⅛ t. pepper

In a saucepan over medium heat, cover asparagus with water. Bring to a boil and cook until crisp-tender, about 4 minutes; drain. In a skillet over medium heat, melt one tablespoon butter. Sauté mushrooms and garlic in butter until tender and moisture has evaporated, 5 to 7 minutes. Add mushroom mixture to asparagus; keep warm. In a bowl, whisk together eggs, milk and seasonings. Melt remaining butter in skillet; swirl to coat bottom and sides. Add egg mixture. As eggs cook, gently lift up edges with a spatula and let uncooked egg run underneath until set. Spoon asparagus mixture onto one half of omelet. Slide omelet onto a plate; fold over. Cut into wedges.

Asparagus & Mushroom Omelet

Anne Muns, *Scottsdale, AZ*

Garden-Fresh Egg Casserole

Fresh tomatoes and spinach turn this breakfast casserole into something extra special! It's perfect for overnight guests.

Serves 8 to 10

18 eggs, beaten
1½ c. shredded Monterey Jack cheese
1 c. buttermilk
1 c. cottage cheese
1 c. spinach, chopped
1 c. tomatoes, chopped
½ c. butter, melted
½ c. onion, grated

Combine all ingredients; pour into a greased 13"x9" baking pan. Cover; refrigerate overnight. Bake, uncovered, at 350 degrees for 50 minutes to one hour.

Judy Mitchell, *Huntley, IL*

Judy's Famous Banana Muffins

Our local newspaper featured me as "Cook of the Week" with this recipe! I found the original recipe many years ago and have revised it over the years. It's a favorite of family & friends.

Makes one dozen

3 very ripe bananas, mashed
2 eggs, beaten
½ c. canola oil
½ c. plus 1 T. sugar, divided
½ c. quick-cooking oats, uncooked
½ c. whole-wheat flour
½ c. all-purpose flour
½ c. wheat germ
1 t. vanilla extract
1 t. baking powder
½ t. baking soda
¼ t. salt
¼ c. chopped walnuts

In a large bowl, stir together bananas, eggs, oil and ½ cup sugar until combined. Add remaining ingredients except walnuts and remaining sugar; stir just until blended. Spoon batter into 12 paper-lined muffin cups, filling about ⅔ full. Sprinkle tops with walnuts and remaining sugar. Bake at 350 degrees for 20 to 25 minutes, until golden and a toothpick tests clean. Let muffins cool in tin for 5 minutes; remove to a wire rack and cool completely.

Judy's Famous Banana Muffins

Susan Brees, *Lincoln, NE*

Tuna Seashell Salad

I took this yummy salad to a potluck party and it won 1st place!

Serves 6 to 8

16-oz. pkg. shell macaroni, uncooked
12-oz. can tuna, drained
3 eggs, hard-boiled, peeled and diced
4-oz. pkg. mild Cheddar cheese, diced
½ to 1 c. mayonnaise-type salad dressing
¼ c. sweet pickle relish

Cook macaroni according to package directions; drain. Rinse macaroni with cold water; drain well. Combine all ingredients in a large serving bowl; chill.

Jo Ann, *Gooseberry Patch*

Pecan-Stuffed Deviled Eggs

Top with fresh parsley sprigs and chopped pecans for a festive presentation.

Serves 6

6 eggs, hard-boiled and peeled
¼ c. mayonnaise
1 t. onion, grated
½ t. fresh parsley, chopped
½ t. dry mustard
⅛ t. salt
⅓ c. pecans, coarsely chopped
Garnish: fresh parsley

Cut eggs in half lengthwise and carefully remove yolks. Mash yolks in a small bowl. Stir in mayonnaise and next 4 ingredients; blend well. Stir in pecans. Spoon or pipe yolk mixture evenly into egg-white halves. Garnish, if desired.

> ~ **Quick Tip** ~
>
> Whip up deviled eggs in no time by combining ingredients in a plastic zipping bag instead of a bowl. Blend by squeezing the bag, then snip off a corner and pipe the filling into the egg white halves.

Pecan-Stuffed Deviled Eggs

Pat Martin, *Riverside, CA*

Icebox Mashed Potatoes

These potatoes are delicious with gravy, but really don't need any topping because they are so creamy and good! A wonderful make-ahead dish that travels well too.

Makes 10 to 12 servings

5 lbs. baking potatoes, peeled and halved
2 cubes chicken bouillon
½ t. garlic salt
2 t. onion powder
2 t. salt
¼ t. pepper
16-oz. container sour cream
8-oz. pkg. cream cheese
2 T. butter, sliced
Optional: additional butter, snipped fresh
    chives

Cover potatoes with water in a deep stockpot; add bouillon and garlic salt. Bring to a boil over high heat; cook until potatoes are tender, about 20 minutes. Remove from heat; drain in a colander. Return potatoes to the same pot and mash. Add onion powder, salt, pepper, sour cream and cream cheese; mix well. Spoon potato mixture into a greased 13"x9" baking pan; dot with butter. Bake, uncovered, at 350 degrees for 40 minutes. If top browns too quickly, cover with aluminum foil for the last 10 minutes. To make ahead, allow unbaked potato mixture to cool slightly; cover with plastic wrap and refrigerate up to 3 days. To serve, let stand at room temperature for 30 minutes; uncover and bake as directed. Garnish as desired.

Nancy Wise, *Little Rock, AR*

Baked Maple Ham

Clove-studded ham makes a stately centerpiece for any meal...especially for Easter. Serve the ham on a platter with wedges of red and green apples for a simple, elegant presentation. With any luck, there'll be plenty of leftover ham for sandwiches.

Serves 16

8 to 9-lb. smoked fully cooked shank ham
whole cloves
1¼ c. brown sugar, packed
½ c. maple syrup

Slice skin from ham. Score top of ham in a diamond pattern, making cuts ⅛-inch deep. Stud with whole cloves. Place ham, fat-side up, on a rack in a shallow roasting pan. Insert a meat thermometer into center of ham, making sure it does not touch bone or fat. Bake at 325 degrees for 2 to 2½ hours or until meat thermometer registers 135 degrees. Combine brown sugar and maple syrup in a small bowl; stir well. Brush brown sugar mixture over ham. Bake 20 to 30 more minutes or until thermometer registers 140 degrees. Remove from oven and let stand 10 minutes before carving.

> ⚊ **Make it Special** ⚊
>
> There's nothing quite like pure maple syrup. In a recipe like this one, where much of the flavor comes from the syrup, we recommend using the real thing. Maple-flavored syrup is a blend of maple syrup and corn syrup, and it lacks the full-bodied flavor of pure maple syrup.

Baked Maple Ham

Rachel Ripley, *Pittsburgh, PA*

Sweet Ambrosia Salad

Kids of all ages love this sweet, creamy salad! I like to serve it for a Mother's Day luncheon with fresh bread and hot tea.

Makes 8 to 10 servings

20-oz. can pineapple chunks, drained
14½-oz. jar maraschino cherries, drained
11-oz. can mandarin oranges, drained
8-oz. container sour cream
10½-oz. pkg. pastel mini marshmallows
½ c. sweetened flaked coconut

Combine fruit in a large bowl; stir in sour cream until coated. Fold in marshmallows and coconut; cover and chill overnight.

Dana Harpster, *Kansas City, MO*

Green Peas with Crispy Bacon

I've used bacon bits and even diced ham in place of the bacon in the recipe. Both worked!

Serves 6

2 slices bacon
1 shallot, sliced
½ t. orange zest
½ c. orange juice
¼ t. salt
½ t. pepper
16-oz. pkg. frozen sweet green peas, thawed
1 t. butter
1 T. fresh mint, chopped
Garnish: fresh mint sprigs

Cook bacon in a skillet over medium heat until crisp. Remove and drain on paper towels, reserving one teaspoon drippings in skillet. Crumble bacon and set aside. Sauté shallot in reserved drippings over medium-high heat for 2 minutes, or until tender. Stir in orange zest, orange juice, salt and pepper. Cook, stirring occasionally, for 5 minutes, or until liquid is reduced by half. Add peas and cook 5 more minutes; stir in butter and chopped mint. Transfer peas to a serving dish and sprinkle with crumbled bacon. Garnish as desired.

⌒ Time-Saving Shortcut ⌒

Rather than chase little round peas around the plate, be sure to serve this side with fluffy biscuits, or "pea pushers," to help you get every pea on your fork.

Green Peas with Crispy Bacon

Lori Rosenberg, *Cleveland, OH*

Spring Ramen Salad

This yummy recipe is truly made to clean out the fridge...you can put almost anything in it!

Makes 4 servings

3-oz. pkg. chicken-flavored ramen noodles
1 t. sesame oil
½ c. seedless grapes, halved
½ c. apple, cored and diced
¼ c. pineapple, diced
2 green onions, diced
1 c. cooked chicken, cubed
1 c. Muenster cheese, cubed
1½ T. lemon juice
⅛ c. canola oil
1 t. sugar
Garnish: sesame seed

Set aside seasoning packet from ramen noodles. Cook noodles according to package directions. Drain noodles; rinse with cold water. In a bowl, toss sesame oil with noodles to coat. Stir in fruit, onions, chicken and cheese. In a separate bowl, whisk together lemon juice, canola oil, sugar and ½ teaspoon of contents of seasoning packet. Pour over noodle mixture; toss to coat. Garnish with sesame seed. Cover and chill before serving.

Crystal Bruns, *Iliff, CO*

Avocado Egg Salad Sandwiches

A fresh and delicious twist on egg salad... serve it on your favorite hearty bread!

Makes 6 sandwiches

6 eggs, hard-boiled, peeled and chopped
2 avocados, halved, pitted and cubed
¼ c. red onion, minced
⅓ c. mayonnaise
1 T. mustard
salt and pepper to taste
12 slices thinly-sliced whole-grain bread

Mash eggs with a fork in a bowl until crumbly. Add remaining ingredients except bread slices. Gently mix together until blended. Spread egg mixture evenly over 6 bread slices. Top with remaining bread slices.

Avocado Egg Salad Sandwiches

Lynn Daniel, *Portage, MI*

Yummy Blue Cheese Burgers

These mouthwatering burgers will be a hit at your next cookout.

Serves 6

2 lbs. ground beef
Cajun seasoning to taste
1 c. half-and-half
1 clove garlic, finely minced
1 t. dried rosemary
1 t. dried basil
4-oz. container crumbled blue cheese
6 kaiser rolls, split, toasted and buttered
Optional: sliced red onion, butter

Form ground beef into 6 patties; sprinkle with Cajun seasoning to taste. Grill to desired doneness. Combine half-and-half, garlic and herbs in a saucepan. Bring to a boil; simmer until thickened and reduced by half. Add blue cheese; stir just until melted. Place burgers on rolls; spoon sauce over burgers. If desired, sauté red onion in butter until tender; spoon onto burgers.

Joshua Logan, *Corpus Christi, TX*

Egg & Bacon Quesadillas

I make these quesadillas on weekends when I have plenty of time to enjoy them. It would also be a great recipe to serve when celebrating Cinco de Mayo. Serve with a cup of yogurt or some fresh fruit.

Serves 4

2 T. butter, divided
4 8-inch flour tortillas
5 eggs, beaten
½ c. skim milk
8-oz. pkg. shredded Cheddar cheese
2 slices bacon, crisply cooked and crumbled
Optional: salsa, plain yogurt

Lightly spread about ¼ teaspoon butter on one side of each tortilla; set aside. In a bowl, beat eggs and milk until combined. Pour egg mixture into a hot, lightly greased skillet; cook and stir over medium heat until done. Remove scrambled eggs to a dish and keep warm. Melt remaining butter in the skillet and add a tortilla, buttered-side down. Layer with ¼ of the cheese, ½ of the eggs and ½ of the bacon. Top with ¼ of the cheese and a tortilla, buttered-side up. Cook about one to 2 minutes on each side, until golden. Repeat with remaining ingredients. Cut each into 4 wedges and serve with salsa and plain yogurt, if desired.

Egg & Bacon Quesadillas

Connie Herek, *Bay City, MI*

Mark's Egg Salad Sandwiches

I must confess...this is my husband's recipe. It's so delicious!

Serves 6 to 8

6 eggs, hard-boiled, peeled and chopped
$\frac{1}{3}$ c. celery, finely chopped
$\frac{1}{3}$ c. onion, finely chopped
3 to 4 T. mayonnaise-type salad dressing
1 to 2 t. mustard
1 t. Worcestershire sauce
$\frac{1}{2}$ t. salt
$\frac{1}{4}$ t. pepper
$\frac{1}{2}$ t. dry mustard
1 T. dill weed
1 loaf sliced bread

Mix all ingredients except bread in a small bowl; refrigerate about one hour. Spread on bread.

Jennifer Oglesby, *Brookville, IN*

Garden-Fresh Pesto Pizza

With this easy pizza, you can really taste what fresh is all about! I came up with this recipe last year when I had a bounty of cherry tomatoes and fresh basil.

Makes 8 servings

1 ready-to-use rectangular pizza crust
$\frac{1}{3}$ c. basil pesto
$\frac{1}{2}$ c. shredded mozzarella cheese
$1\frac{1}{2}$ c. cherry tomatoes, halved
Optional: 4 leaves fresh basil

Place crust on sheet pan, lightly greased with non-stick vegetable spray if directed on package. Spread pesto over pizza crust and top with cheese. Scatter tomatoes over cheese; add a basil leaf to each quarter of the pizza, if desired. Bake at 425 degrees for about 8 to 10 minutes, until crust is crisp and cheese is lightly golden. Cut into wedges or squares.

Garden-Fresh Pesto Pizza

Gail Blain, *Stockton, KS*

Ham Steak & Apples Skillet

My grandmother's old black cast-iron skillet brings back wonderful memories of the delicious things she used to make in it.

Serves 6

3 T. butter
½ c. brown sugar, packed
1 T. Dijon mustard
2 c. apples, cored and diced
2 1-lb. bone-in ham steaks

Melt butter in a large skillet over medium heat. Add brown sugar and mustard; bring to a simmer. Add apples; cover and simmer for 5 minutes. Top apples with ham steaks. Cover with a lid; simmer for about 10 more minutes or until apples are tender. Remove ham to a platter and cut into serving-size pieces. Top ham with apples and sauce.

Liz Plotnick-Snay, *Gooseberry Patch*

Mitchell's Wonderful Brisket

Treat your family & friends to this amazing brisket during Passover. It bakes in the oven for several hours, giving you plenty of time to relax and enjoy your guests.

Serves 10 to 12

5-lb. beef brisket
salt and pepper to taste
1 t. garlic powder
1 onion, sliced
1 bay leaf
10 to 12 whole cloves
¾ c. chili sauce
1 T. Worcestershire sauce
½ c. water
¼ c. brown sugar, packed
½ t. paprika

Sprinkle all sides of brisket with salt, pepper and garlic powder. Place in an ungreased 13"x9" baking pan. Lay sliced onion and bay leaf on top of brisket. Cover and refrigerate for 2 to 3 hours. Bake brisket, covered, at 300 degrees for 3 hours. Remove from oven and evenly stick cloves into brisket. In a bowl, combine remaining ingredients. Stir to mix well; pour over brisket. Bake for one hour longer. Remove bay leaf and cloves; slice to serve.

Mitchell's Wonderful Brisket

Regina Kostyu, *Delaware, OH*

Special Deviled Eggs

These pretty little eggs are anything but devilish to make. You'll love them!

Makes 2 dozen

1 doz. eggs, hard-boiled and peeled
3 to 4 T. coleslaw dressing
⅛ to ¼ t. garlic salt with parsley
Garnish: paprika, snipped fresh chives

Slice eggs in half lengthwise; scoop yolks into a bowl. Arrange whites on a serving platter; set aside. Mash yolks well with a fork. Stir in dressing to desired consistency and add garlic salt to taste. Spoon or pipe yolk mixture into whites. Garnish as desired; chill.

Judy Renkievich, *Grand Marais, MN*

Rosemary-Lemon Scones

Fresh rosemary and lemon zest are the secret ingredients in these flaky scones.

Makes 8

2 c. all-purpose flour
2 T. sugar
1 T. baking powder
2 t. fresh rosemary, chopped
2 t. lemon zest
¼ t. salt
¼ c. butter
2 eggs
½ c. whipping cream
Garnish: additional whipping cream,
**   additional sugar**

Combine first 6 ingredients in a large mixing bowl. With a pastry blender or 2 knives, cut in butter until mixture is crumbly. Combine eggs and whipping cream in a medium bowl; add to flour mixture and stir well. (Dough may be sticky.) Knead dough lightly 4 times on a well-floured surface. Shape dough into an 8-inch circle about ½-inch thick. Place dough on a lightly greased baking sheet. Cut circle into wedges; do not separate wedges. Brush additional cream over top of scones and sprinkle with additional sugar. Bake scones at 425 degrees for 14 minutes or until golden.

> **⟨ Cooking How-to ⟩**
>
> When making scones, don't strive for a smooth dough; it should be rough. Be sure to use cold butter, working quickly with it and doing very little mixing...your mixture should be crumbly. Pat dough into a circle rather than rolling it into shape.

Rosemary-Lemon Scones

Megan Brooks, *Antioch, TN*

After-Church Egg Muffins

I whip these up for my boys almost every Sunday after church. They are perfect for the Easter holiday.

Makes 4 servings

10¾-oz. can Cheddar cheese soup
1½ c. milk
4 eggs
4 English muffins, split and toasted
3 T. butter, divided
4 slices Canadian bacon

In a bowl, mix together soup and milk. Fill 4 greased custard cups ¼ full with soup mixture. Set cups on a baking sheet. Crack an egg into each cup, being careful not to break the yolks. Bake cups at 350 degrees for 12 minutes. Meanwhile, cook bacon until crisp . Top each muffin half with one teaspoon butter. Place 4 muffin halves on a baking sheet. Top each with a slice of bacon. Turn out a baked egg onto each bacon-topped muffin half. Drizzle remaining cheese sauce over each egg. Top with other halves of muffins. Bake for an additional 2 minutes, or until heated through.

Linda Bonwill. *Englewood, FL*

Spinach & Tomato French Toast

A healthier way to make French toast...plus, it looks so pretty!

Serves 4

3 eggs
salt and pepper to taste
8 slices Italian bread
4 c. fresh spinach, torn
2 tomatoes
sliced shaved Parmesan cheese

In a bowl, beat eggs with salt and pepper. Dip bread slices into egg. Place in a lightly greased skillet over medium heat; cook one side until lightly golden. Place fresh spinach, tomato slice and cheese onto each slice, pressing lightly to secure. Flip and briefly cook on other side until cooked. Flip over and serve open-face.

Spinach & Tomato French Toast

Janice Woods, *Northern Cambria, PA*

Chilled Melon Soup

This tasty and beautiful recipe is perfect for summer get-togethers with friends.

Makes 4 to 6 servings

3 c. cantaloupe melon, peeled, seeded and
    chopped
2 T. sugar, divided
¼ c. orange juice, divided
⅛ t. salt, divided
3 c. honeydew melon, peeled, seeded and
    chopped
Garnish: fresh mint sprigs or orange slices

In a blender, process cantaloupe, half the sugar, half the juice and half the salt until smooth. Cover and refrigerate. Repeat with honeydew and remaining ingredients except garnish. Refrigerate, covered, in separate containers. To serve, pour equal amounts of each mixture at the same time on opposite sides of individual soup bowls. Garnish as desired.

Lizzy Burnley, *Ankeny, IA*

Lizzy's Make-Ahead Egg Casserole

This recipe is a favorite for breakfast, lunch or dinner. And preparing it ahead makes it that much easier! It is perfect for serving after the Easter egg hunt or for a Mother's Day brunch.

Serves 12

1 doz. eggs, beaten
1 c. cooked ham, diced
3 c. whole milk
12 frozen waffles, divided
2 c. shredded Cheddar cheese, divided

In a large bowl, beat eggs. Stir in ham and milk. Grease a 13"x9" baking pan. Place one layer of waffles in the bottom of the pan. Pour half of the mixture on the waffles. Sprinkle with half of the cheese. Continue layering waffles, egg mixture and cheese. Cover and refrigerate overnight. Uncover and bake at 350 degrees for about one hour or until eggs are set.

Lizzy's Make-Ahead Egg Casserole

Jenna Fowls, *Warsaw, OH*

Grandma's Wilted Lettuce

An old-fashioned favorite! To save time, heat the water, vinegar, sugar and drippings in a mug in the microwave.

Makes 6 servings

2 heads leaf lettuce, torn
Optional: ⅛ t. salt, ⅛ t. pepper
2 eggs, hard-boiled, peeled and quartered
Optional: 2 green onions, sliced
4 to 6 slices bacon
¼ c. vinegar
2 T. water
1 T. sugar

Arrange lettuce in a salad bowl; season with salt and pepper, if desired. Add eggs and green onions, if using. Toss to combine; set aside. Meanwhile, in a cast-iron skillet over medium-high heat, cook bacon until crisp. Remove bacon to a paper towel; reserve drippings in skillet. Add vinegar, water and sugar to drippings in skillet. Heat to boiling, stirring until sugar dissolves. Pour over salad; toss again. Top with crumbled bacon and serve immediately.

Debby Horton, *Cincinnati, OH*

Easy Italian Wedding Soup

Though you probably won't see this dish on the menu at many weddings, it is a traditional Italian soup that's often served for holidays and other special events.

Serves 4

2 14½-oz. cans chicken broth
1 c. water
1 c. medium shell pasta, uncooked
16 frozen meatballs, cooked
2 c. fresh spinach, finely shredded
1 c. pizza sauce

Bring broth and one cup water to a boil in a large saucepan over medium-high heat; add pasta and meatballs. Return to a boil; cook for 7 to 9 minutes, until pasta is tender. Do not drain. Reduce heat; stir in spinach and pizza sauce. Cook for one to 2 minutes, until heated through.

Easy Italian Wedding Soup

Melody Taynor, *Everett, WA*

Chilled Apple & Cheese Salad

As a girl, I was convinced that I didn't like gelatin salads. But when my Aunt Clara served this at an anniversary party, I found I had been mistaken!

Makes 6 servings

3-oz. pkg. lemon gelatin mix
1 c. boiling water
¾ c. cold water
⅔ c. red apple, cored and finely chopped
⅓ c. shredded Cheddar cheese
¼ c. celery, chopped

In a bowl, dissolve gelatin in boiling water. Stir in cold water; chill until partially set. Fold in remaining ingredients. Pour into a 3-cup mold. Cover and chill 3 hours, or until firm. Unmold onto a serving plate.

Kelley Nicholson, *Gooseberry Patch*

Arugula Potato Cornugula

A fast and easy recipe. Let your kids help you toss in the ingredients one by one, and with each ingredient come up with a silly word that rhymes with arugula. They're sure to give this side dish a try!

Makes 4 servings

2 T. butter
1 t. garlic, minced
6 new redskin potatoes, sliced
¼ t. salt
¼ t. pepper
1 c. frozen corn
½ c. frozen lima beans
1 c. fresh arugula, torn
salt and pepper to taste

Melt butter in a large skillet over medium heat; cook garlic until tender. Stir in potatoes and seasoning. Cover and cook until tender, about 10 minutes, turning occasionally. Add corn and beans; cook until potatoes are tender, about 8 to 10 minutes. Season with salt and pepper. Add arugula; cover and let stand until arugula is wilted.

Arugula Potato Cornugula

Leslie Stimel, *Columbus, Ohio*

Greek Orzo Salad

This salad is my own creation...feel free to add or subtract any of these ingredients to suit your own taste!

Serves 4

⅓ c. roasted red peppers, diced
¼ c. kalamata olives, sliced
1 tomato, diced
2 c. orzo pasta, cooked
½ c. crumbled feta cheese
balsamic vinegar to taste

Combine peppers, olives and tomato in a medium bowl; set aside. Rinse orzo with cold water; drain well. Add orzo and feta cheese to pepper mixture; mix well. Drizzle with vinegar; stir again. Serve warm or chilled.

Amanda Homan, *Columbus, OH*

Tarragon Steak Dinner Salad

Delicious...a perfect light spring meal.

Serves 4

6 c. Boston lettuce
2 pears, cored, peeled and sliced
½ red onion, thinly sliced
½ lb. grilled beef steak, thinly sliced
¼ c. crumbled blue cheese
½ c. red wine vinaigrette salad dressing
1 T. fresh tarragon, minced
¼ t. pepper

Arrange lettuce, pears and onion on 4 serving plates. Top with sliced steak and sprinkle with cheese. Combine dressing, tarragon and pepper in a small bowl; whisk well. Drizzle dressing mixture over salad.

Anita Williams, *Pikeville, KY*

Fresh Fruit Kabobs & Poppy Seed Dip

Try grilling these kabobs for a new spin. Place skewers over medium-high heat for 3 to 5 minutes...yum!

Makes 8 to 10 servings

6 c. fresh fruit like strawberries, kiwi, pineapple, honeydew and cantaloupe, peeled and cut into bite-size cubes or slices
8 to 10 wooden skewers

Arrange fruit pieces alternately on skewers. Serve Poppy Seed Dip alongside fruit kabobs.

POPPY SEED DIP:

1 c. vanilla yogurt
2 T. honey
4 t. lime juice
1 t. vanilla extract
1 t. poppy seed

Stir together ingredients in a small bowl. Keep chilled.

Fresh Fruit Kabobs & Poppy Seed Dip

Peter Kay, *Phoenixville, PA*

Easy-Peasy Berry Cake

This is the easiest berry cake you can make. It's a great spur-of-the moment dessert and it looks so good, they will think you worked all day on it. Top it with fresh whipped cream and additional berries for a wonderful dessert, or serve as is with a steaming cup of coffee or tea.

Makes 8 servings

½ c. butter, room temperature
¾ c. plus 1 T. sugar, divided
3 eggs
2 t. baking powder
1 c. plus 1 t. all-purpose flour, divided
1 c. favorite berries, stems removed

In a large bowl, blend butter and ¾ cup sugar. Add eggs, one at a time, beating after each egg. Add baking powder and one cup flour; stir until smooth. Pour batter into a greased 10" round cake pan or springform pan. Lightly dust berries with remaining flour. Scatter berries over batter and sprinkle with remaining sugar. Bake at 350 degrees for about 40 minutes, testing for doneness with a wooden toothpick.

Anna McMaster, *Portland, OR*

Easter Ice Cream Sandwiches

Wrap these springtime treats in pastel-colored plastic wrap and store in the freezer until ready to serve.

Makes about one dozen

2 c. butter, softened
1⅓ c. sugar
2 eggs, beaten
2 t. vanilla extract
5 c. all-purpose flour
assorted food colorings
1 pt. vanilla ice cream, softened
Optional: 2 c. sweetened flaked coconut

Blend butter and sugar together; stir in eggs and vanilla. Add flour; mix until well blended. Shape into a ball; cover and chill for 4 hours to overnight. Reserve one tablespoon of dough for each color. Roll out remaining dough on a floured surface ¼-inch thick. Use a 3-inch egg-shaped cookie cutter to cut dough. Tint reserved dough with food coloring as desired. Form colored dough into small balls and ropes and arrange on half the cookies. Place on ungreased baking sheets. Bake at 350 degrees for 7 to 9 minutes. Cool on baking sheets one minute; remove cookies to cool completely on wire rack. Position plain cookie on bottom, spread with ice cream and top with decorated cookie. Gently press together; freeze until serving time. If desired, mix a few drops of green food coloring and coconut; let dry on wax paper. Place cookies on colored coconut.

Easter Ice Cream Sandwiches

Gladys Kielar, *Whitehouse, OH*

California Pita Sandwiches

Our family loves any kind of pita sandwich. When we were in California we had this sandwich at a restaurant. When we got back, I made them for us and now we have them all the time.

Makes 2 sandwiches

1 pita round, halved and split
1 avocado, halved, pitted and sliced
1 tomato, sliced
1 slice Swiss cheese, halved
several leaves Romaine lettuce
Thousand Island salad dressing to taste

Fill each half of pita with avocado, tomato, cheese, lettuce leaves and dressing to taste.

Cheri Maxwell, *Gulf Breeze, FL*

Caribbean Chicken Salad

Try grilling the chicken on a countertop grill for a different flavor.

Serves 4

$\frac{1}{2}$ c. honey-mustard salad dressing
1 t. lime zest
4 boneless, skinless chicken breasts
1 T. Jamaican jerk seasoning
1 T. oil
2 10-oz. pkgs. mixed salad greens
2 mangoes, peeled, pitted and diced

Stir together salad dressing and lime zest; cover and chill. Sprinkle chicken with seasoning. Heat oil over medium heat in a large skillet. Add chicken; cook 6 minutes per side until golden and no longer pink. Slice chicken thinly. Arrange salad greens on 4 plates; top with chicken and mangoes. Drizzle with dressing.

Anne Alesauskas, *Minocqua, WI*

Avocado Feta Dip

My family doesn't care for tomatoes but we love red peppers...so we love this!

Makes 3 cups, serves 12

2 avocados, halved, pitted and diced
$\frac{3}{4}$ c. crumbled feta cheese
1 red pepper, diced
1 green onion, thinly sliced
1 T. lemon juice
2 t. dill weed
$\frac{1}{4}$ t. salt
$\frac{1}{4}$ t. pepper

Combine all ingredients in a serving bowl; mix until well blended.

Avocado Feta Dip

Beth Flack, *Terre Haute, IN*

Caprese Salad

Very refreshing! This is one of my favorite summer salads. Try it with cherry tomatoes and mini mozzarella balls too.

Serves 6

2 beefsteak tomatoes, sliced
4-oz. pkg. fresh mozzarella cheese, sliced
8 leaves fresh basil
Italian salad dressing to taste

Layer tomatoes, cheese slices and basil leaves in rows or in a circle around a large platter. Sprinkle with salad dressing. Cover and chill for one hour before serving.

Chris Taylor, *Bountiful, UT*

Ryan's Yummy Pasta Salad

My picky ten-year-old's favorite salad!

Serves 6 to 8

8-oz. pkg. refrigerated cheese tortellini, uncooked
2½ c. rotelle pasta, uncooked
1 c. frozen mixed vegetables
1 c. deli roast chicken, chopped
2 T. lemon pepper, or to taste
ranch salad dressing to taste

In separate saucepans, cook tortellini and rotelle according to package directions, adding frozen vegetables to pasta pan. Drain; combine in a large serving bowl. Add chicken to pasta; sprinkle generously with lemon pepper. Add salad dressing to desired consistency and toss to mix. May be served warm or chilled.

Deanna Smith, *Huntington, WV*

BLT Bites

A favorite sandwich becomes an appetizer! Use heirloom tomatoes in different colors for a stunning presentation for a spring buffet.

Makes 10 servings

20 large cherry tomatoes
4 slices bacon, crisply cooked and crumbled
½ c. light mayonnaise
⅓ c. green onion, chopped
3 T. grated Parmesan cheese
2 T. fresh parsley, finely chopped

Cut a thin slice off the top of each tomato; scoop out and discard pulp. Invert tomatoes onto a paper towel to drain. Combine the remaining ingredients in a small bowl; mix well. Spoon mixture into each tomato; refrigerate for several hours before serving.

BLT Bites

Sharon Jones, *Oklahoma City, OK*

Spinach & Clementine Salad

This fresh, crunchy salad is a perfect salad to serve at an Easter breakfast.

Makes 8 servings

2 lbs. clementines, peeled and sectioned
2 16-oz. pkgs. baby spinach
4 stalks celery, thinly sliced on the diagonal
1 c. red onion, thinly sliced
½ c. pine nuts or walnuts, toasted
¼ c. dried cherries
2 T. red wine vinegar
¼ c. olive oil
1 t. Dijon mustard
1 clove garlic, minced
⅛ t. sugar
salt and pepper to taste

In a large salad bowl, combine clementines, spinach, celery, onion, nuts and cherries. Toss to mix well. Whisk together remaining ingredients in a small bowl; drizzle over salad. Serve immediately.

Lisanne Miller, *Canton, MS*

Sun-Dried Tomato Toasties

These are so quick to make and are so pretty to serve. I serve them on a wood serving tray while they are still warm.

Makes 2 to 3 dozen

½ c. sun-dried tomato and olive relish
2¼-oz. can chopped black olives, drained
2 t. garlic, chopped
8-oz. pkg. shredded mozzarella cheese, divided
1 loaf French bread, thinly sliced

Mix together relish, olives, garlic and ¼ cup cheese; spread evenly on bread slices. Arrange bread on an ungreased baking sheet; sprinkle the bread pieces with remaining cheese. Bake at 300 degrees for 4 to 5 minutes, until cheese melts; serve immediately.

Sun-Dried Tomato Toasties

Debra Elliott, *Birmingham, AL*

Pineapple Pudding

This pineapple pudding is my favorite. It's an easy-to-make, mouthwatering dessert that will tickle your taste buds.

Serves 6

12-oz. pkg. vanilla wafers, divided
⅓ c. sugar
3 T. cornstarch
¼ t. salt
2½ c. milk
1½ t. vanilla extract
20-oz. can crushed pineapple, drained
8-oz. container frozen whipped topping,
    thawed
Garnish: pineapple slices, maraschino
    cherries

Layer wafers in a large glass trifle bowl until bottom is covered, reserving 8 to 10 for garnish. In a saucepan over medium heat, combine sugar, cornstarch and salt. Stir in milk. Cook, stirring occasionally, until mixture thickens. Add vanilla and cook for 2 to 3 minutes. Once mixture is thick, fold in crushed pineapple. Spread pudding mixture over wafers in bowl; let cool. Top pudding with whipped topping. Garnish with pineapple slices, reserved wafers and cherries.

Vickie, *Gooseberry Patch*

Caramel Cake

This cake looks so spring-like. I serve it on Mother's Day because I love it!

Serves 8

8-oz. container sour cream
¼ c. milk
1 c. butter, softened
2 c. sugar
4 eggs
2¾ c. all-purpose flour
2 t. baking powder
½ t. salt
1 t. vanilla extract

Combine sour cream and milk; set aside. Beat butter at medium speed with an electric mixer until creamy. Gradually add sugar, beating well. Add eggs, one at a time, beating until blended. Combine flour, baking powder and salt; add to butter mixture alternately with sour cream mixture, beginning and ending with flour mixture. Beat at medium-low speed until blended after each addition. Stir in vanilla. Pour batter into 2 greased and floured 9" round cake pans. Bake at 350 degrees for 30 to 35 minutes or until a toothpick inserted comes out clean. Cool in pans on wire racks 10 minutes. Remove from pans; cool one hour or until completely cool. Spread Whipped Cream Caramel Frosting between layers, on top and sides.

WHIPPED CREAM CARAMEL FROSTING:

1 c. butter
2 c. dark brown sugar, packed
¼ c. plus 2 T. whipping cream
2 t. vanilla extract
3¾ c. powdered sugar

Melt butter in a 3-quart saucepan over medium heat. Add brown sugar; bring to a boil, stirring constantly. Stir in whipping cream and vanilla; bring to a boil. Remove from heat; cool one hour. Transfer to a mixing bowl. Sift powdered sugar into frosting. Beat at high speed with an electric mixer until creamy and spreading consistency.

Caramel Cake

Dianne Gregory, *Sheridan, AR*

Cappuccino Cooler

A perfect beverage to serve after dinner!

Makes 4 servings

1½ c. brewed coffee, cooled
1½ c. chocolate ice cream, softened
¼ c. chocolate syrup
crushed ice
Garnish: frozen whipped topping, thawed

Blend coffee, ice cream and syrup together until smooth; set aside. Fill 4 glasses ¾ full with crushed ice; pour in coffee mixture. Top each with a dollop of whipped topping. Serve immediately.

Darci Stavish, *Randall, MN*

Strawberry Pie

Take the whole family strawberry picking... not only is it fun, but you'll have this fresh, homemade pie to enjoy too!

Makes 8 to 10 servings

1 c. all-purpose flour
2 T. powdered sugar
½ c. butter, softened
1½ c. water
¾ c. sugar
⅛ t. salt
2 T. cornstarch
3-oz. pkg. strawberry gelatin mix
4 c. strawberries, hulled and halved
Optional: whipped topping

Combine flour and powdered sugar; cut butter into flour mixture until dough resembles coarse crumbs. Pat into a 9" pie plate; bake at 350 degrees for 15 minutes. Set aside to cool. In a 2-quart saucepan, bring water, sugar, salt and cornstarch to a boil until clear; stir in gelatin until dissolved. Remove from heat; cool slightly. Pour ¼ of the gelatin mixture into pie crust. Fill crust with strawberries; pour remaining gelatin mixture over the top. Chill in refrigerator until set; serve with whipped topping, if desired.

Strawberry Pie

Jennifer Gutermuth, *Oshkosh, WI*

Veggie, Egg & Rice Breakfast Bowls

I love eating veggies for breakfast! I use whatever is in my kitchen...red pepper, zucchini, green beans. They are all good in this bowl. And of course the asparagus makes the bowl perfect for a spring meal.

Makes 4 servings

1 T. olive oil
1 lb. asparagus, cut into bite-sized pieces
3 c. fresh spinach leaves
3 c. cabbage, shredded
1½ c. cooked brown rice, warmed
½ c. hummus
1 avocado, peeled, pitted and diced
4 eggs
Garnish: chopped pecans, pumpkin seeds

Heat oil in a skillet over medium-high heat. Add asparagus and sauté for 4 to 5 minutes, stirring occasionally, until tender; set side. In a separate bowl, combine spinach and Honey-Mustard Dressing. Add asparagus, cabbage and rice; toss until combined. Divide spinach mixture evenly among 4 bowls. Top each with hummus and avocado; set aside. To poach eggs, fill a skillet with water and bring to a simmer over medium-high heat. Swirl water with a spoon and gently slide in each egg from a saucer. Cook until set, about 2 minutes. Use a slotted spoon to remove each egg to a bowl. Garnish as desired.

HONEY-MUSTARD DRESSING:

2 T. olive oil
2 T. lemon juice
2 t. mustard
2 T. honey
1 clove garlic, minced
salt and pepper to taste

In a small bowl, whisk together all ingredients.

> ~ **Presentation** ~
>
> When serving a one-bowl meal, it makes a good presentation if the recipe is served in low, shallow bowls so the textures and the colors of the ingredients can be seen and enjoyed as well as tasted.

Veggie, Egg & Rice Breakfast Bowls

Charlene Smith, *Lombard, IL*

Coconut Clouds

For extra sparkle, top with a candied cherry and sprinkle with sugar before baking.

Makes 15 to 20

¾ c. sugar
2½ c. flaked coconut
2 egg whites, beaten
1 t. vanilla extract
⅛ t. salt

Combine ingredients together. Beat with an electric mixer on medium-high speed until soft peaks form. Drop by tablespoonfuls, one inch apart, on a greased baking sheet; bake at 350 degrees for 15 to 20 minutes. Cool on a wire rack. Store in an airtight container.

Steven Wilson, *Chesterfield, VA*

Strawberry Layer Cake

Growing up in North Carolina, spring meant strawberry time, Grandma always baked this delicious cake for the Sunday night church social.

Serves 12

6-oz. pkg. strawberry gelatin mix
½ c. hot water
18½-oz. pkg. white cake mix
2 T. all-purpose flour
1 c. strawberries, hulled and chopped
4 eggs
Garnish: fresh strawberries

In a large bowl, dissolve dry gelatin mix in hot water; cool. Add dry cake mix, flour and strawberries; mix well. Add eggs, one at a time, beating slightly after each one. Pour batter into 3 greased 8" round cake pans. Bake at 350 degrees for 20 minutes, or until cake tests done with a toothpick. Cool; assemble layers with Frosting. Garnish with strawberries.

STRAWBERRY FROSTING:

¼ c. butter, softened
3¾ to 5 c. powdered sugar
⅓ c. strawberries, hulled and finely chopped

Blend butter and powdered sugar together, adding powdered sugar to desired consistency. Add chopped strawberries; blend thoroughly.

Strawberry Layer Cake

Linda Lewanski, *Cosby, TN*

Easiest-Ever Cheesecake

You can also drizzle melted chocolate on top for a rich and flavorful twist. Friends will think you spent hours on this simple cheesecake. This makes a great dessert for a spring party.

Serves 12 to 15

12-oz. pkg. vanilla wafers, crushed
1 c. plus 2 T. sugar, divided
½ c. butter, melted
2 8-oz. pkgs. cream cheese, softened
12-oz. container frozen whipped topping,
   thawed
Optional: fresh raspberries

Combine the vanilla wafers, 2 tablespoons sugar and butter; press into the bottom of a 13"x9" baking pan. In a separate bowl, blend together remaining sugar and cream cheese; fold in whipped topping. Spread over wafer crust; chill until firm. Garnish with fresh raspberries, if desired.

Holly Curry, *Middleburgh, NY*

Poppy Seed Cake

The glaze drizzled over this simple cake sets it apart from other poppy seed cakes.

Serves 8 to 10

18¼-oz. pkg. yellow cake mix
1 c. oil
1 c. sour cream
½ c. sugar
4 eggs, beaten
¼ c. poppy seed

In a large bowl, beat together dry cake mix and all remaining ingredients. Pour into a greased and floured Bundt® pan. Bake at 325 degrees for one hour, or until a toothpick inserted tests clean. Turn cake out onto a serving plate. Drizzle Glaze over top.

GLAZE:

½ c. sugar
¼ c. orange juice
½ t. almond extract
½ t. imitation butter flavor
½ t. vanilla extract

Combine all ingredients; mix well.

Poppy Seed Cake

Chapter Four

Summer Celebrations

County fairs, outdoor celebrations, family reunions... summer is a time to relax and have fun together. Get out the grill and cook Firecracker Grilled Salmon to serve with fresh green beans. Finish the meal with a light Fruity Fresh Sorbet. Use the herbs in your garden to make That Yummy Bread to serve with any summer meal. Looking for a show-stopping dessert for that Fourth of July celebration? Whip up a batch of Patriotic Cupcakes that are sure to wow them all! So sit back, relax and enjoy the warm days of summer with recipes that will keep them smiling all season long.

Tiffani Schulte, *Wyandotte, MI*

Blue-Ribbon Corn Dog Bake

This casserole is oh-so easy and it really does taste like a county fair corn dog!

Serves 6

⅓ c. sugar
1 egg, beaten
1 c. all-purpose flour
¾ T. baking powder
½ t. salt
½ c. yellow cornmeal
½ T. butter, melted
¾ c. milk
16-oz. pkg. hot dogs, sliced into bite-size pieces

In a small bowl, mix together sugar and egg. In a separate bowl, mix together flour, baking powder and salt. Add flour mixture to sugar mixture. Add cornmeal, butter and milk, stirring just to combine. Fold in hot dog pieces. Pour into a well-greased 8"x8" baking pan. Bake, uncovered, at 375 degrees for about 15 minutes, or until a toothpick inserted near the center comes out clean.

Rita Miller, *Lincolnwood, IL*

Arugula & Nectarine Salad

We love the combination of the spicy arugula and the sweet nectarines. The walnuts add the perfect crunch!

Makes 4 servings

¼ c. balsamic vinegar
1 T. Dijon mustard
1 T. honey
¼ t. salt
pepper to taste
¼ c. extra-virgin olive oil
¼ lb. fresh arugula, torn
2 ripe nectarines, halved, pitted and sliced
¾ c. chopped walnuts
½ c. crumbled feta cheese

Combine vinegar, mustard, honey, salt and pepper in a shaker jar. Add oil; shake until blended. Divide arugula among 4 salad plates; arrange nectarine slices over arugula. Sprinkle with walnuts and cheese; drizzle with salad dressing to taste.

Arugula & Nectarine Salad

Vickie, *Gooseberry Patch*

Barbecued Pork Chops

Let these chops cook in the oven while you get the picnic tables ready for a fun outdoor party. Just add a salad and lemonade and you are all set!

Makes 8 servings

8 pork chops
3 T. oil
½ c. catsup
⅓ c. vinegar
1 c. water
1 t. celery seed
½ t. nutmeg
1 bay leaf
salt and pepper to taste

In a large skillet over medium heat, brown chops in oil. Drain; arrange chops in a greased 13"x9" baking pan. Combine remaining ingredients except salt and pepper and pour over chops. Cover with aluminum foil. Bake at 325 degrees for 1½ hours, until tender. Discard bay leaf before serving. Add salt and pepper to taste.

Roger Dahlstrom, *Ankeny, IA*

Hickory-Smoked Kabobs

These beautiful kabobs will be the hit of your summer celebration!

Serves 8

1½ lbs. beef top sirloin steak, cut into 1½-inch cubes
8-oz. bottle Russian salad dressing
¼ c. hickory-smoked Worcestershire sauce
1 t. smoke-flavored cooking sauce
½ t. pepper
2 red onions, cut into 1-inch wedges
12 mushrooms, stems trimmed
1 green pepper, cut into 1½-inch pieces
1 red pepper, cut into 1½-inch pieces
3 lemons, cut into wedges
8 14-inch skewers

Place beef in a shallow dish. Combine dressing and next 3 ingredients; stir well. Pour mixture over beef. Cover and marinate in refrigerator 8 hours; stir occasionally. Cook onions in boiling water to cover 2 minutes; drain. Remove beef from marinade, reserving marinade. Bring reserved marinade to a boil. Alternate beef, onions, mushrooms, pepper pieces and lemon wedges on skewers. Grill, covered, over medium-high heat (350 to 400 degrees) 6 minutes on each side or to desired degree of doneness, basting frequently with reserved marinade. Squeeze lemon wedges over kabobs before serving, if desired.

Hickory-Smoked Kabobs

Dee Ann Ice, *Delaware, OH*

Delicious BBQ Hamburgers

If you don't want to get out the grill but are hungry for a burger, these hamburgers are perfect for you!

Serves 4 to 6

1 lb. ground beef
1/2 c. milk
1/2 c. bread crumbs
1/4 t. pepper
1/4 t. garlic powder
1/2 c. onion, chopped
1/2 c. green pepper, chopped
1 c. catsup
2 t. vinegar
2 t. mustard
1/2 c. sugar
3/4 t. salt

Combine beef, milk, bread crumbs, pepper, garlic powder, onion and green pepper; mix well. Shape into patties and place in a skillet; brown both sides. Place in a greased 13"x9" baking pan; set aside. Combine catsup and remaining ingredients in a mixing bowl; pour over patties. Bake at 350 degrees for one hour.

Abby Snay, *San Francisco, CA*

Chicken Taco Salad

We love this salad for a quick meal on summer evenings. It is fun to make!

Makes 8 servings

8 6-inch flour tortillas
2 c. cooked chicken breast, shredded
2 t. taco seasoning mix
1/2 c. water
2 c. lettuce, shredded
1/2 c. black beans, drained and rinsed
1 c. shredded Cheddar cheese
1/2 c. green onion, sliced
1/2 c. canned corn, drained
2 1/4-oz. can sliced black olives, drained
1/2 avocado, pitted, peeled and cubed
Garnish: fresh salsa

Microwave tortillas on high setting for one minute, or until softened. Press each tortilla into an ungreased muffin cup to form a bowl shape. Bake at 350 degrees for 10 minutes; cool. Combine chicken, taco seasoning and water in a skillet over medium heat. Cook, stirring frequently, until blended, about 5 minutes. Divide lettuce among tortilla bowls. Top with chicken and other ingredients, garnishing with salsa.

Chicken Taco Salad

Julie Ann Perkins, *Anderson, IN*

Fresh Corn Salad

Use Silver Queen or another sweet corn variety for this sugary-sweet salad with an oil and vinegar dressing. Using corn freshly cut from the cob yields the sweetest kernels.

Makes 6 cups

6 ears white or yellow corn, husks removed
¼ c. sugar
¼ c. cider vinegar
¼ c. olive oil
½ t. salt
½ t. pepper
1 red onion, diced
1 red pepper, diced
¼ c. fresh parsley, coarsely chopped

Cook corn in boiling salted water in a large stockpot 3 to 4 minutes; drain. Plunge corn into ice water to stop the cooking process; drain. Cut kernels from cobs. Whisk together sugar and next 4 ingredients in a large bowl; add corn, onion, pepper and parsley, tossing to coat. Cover and chill at least 2 hours.

Alma Evans, *Patrick, FL*

Chunky Tomato-Avocado Salad

Let this flavorful salad sit for at least two hours if you don't have time to refrigerate it overnight. The flavors blend together so beautifully!

Serves 4

1 avocado, pitted, peeled and cubed
3 plum tomatoes, chopped
½ c. sweet onion, chopped
1 T. fresh cilantro, chopped
2 to 3 T. lemon juice

Gently stir together all ingredients; cover and refrigerate overnight.

⌒ **A New Twist** ⌒

Use old serving dishes in a new way for a fresh look. Handed-down cream-and-sugar sets can hold sauces, bread sticks can be arranged in gravy boats and a trifle dish can make a great salad bowl.

Chunky Tomato-Avocado Salad

Sonya Labbe, *Los Angeles, CA*

Tomato-Basil Couscous Salad

Everyone seems to love this salad. I think it is the combination of the couscous, basil and tomatoes.

Makes 6 servings

2 c. water
1½ c. couscous, uncooked
1 c. tomatoes, chopped
¼ c. fresh basil, thinly sliced
½ c. olive oil
⅓ c. balsamic vinegar
½ t. salt
¼ t. pepper

In a saucepan over high heat, bring water to a boil. Stir in uncooked couscous; remove from heat. Cover and let stand for 5 minutes, until water is absorbed. Add remaining ingredients and toss to mix. Cover and chill for several hours to overnight.

Regina Wickline, *Pebble Beach, CA*

Grilled Market Veggies

Your friends will be impressed when it is your turn to grill next time when you serve this beautiful and easy veggie dish!

Makes 6 servings

3 zucchini, sliced ¾-inch thick
3 yellow squash, sliced ¾-inch thick
1 baby eggplant, sliced ¾-inch thick
1 sweet onion, sliced ¾-inch thick
2 tomatoes, sliced 1-inch thick
½ c. balsamic vinegar
⅛ c. canola oil
2 cloves garlic, minced
1 T. fresh rosemary, minced
1 T. fresh oregano, chopped
1 T. fresh basil, chopped
1 T. fresh parsley, minced
1 t. sugar
¼ t. salt
¼ t. pepper

Combine vegetables in a large bowl. Whisk together remaining ingredients and pour over vegetables. Toss to coat. Marinate for 30 minutes to one hour. Remove vegetables from marinade with a slotted spoon. Arrange on a grill over medium-hot heat. Grill 2 to 5 minutes on each side, basting often with marinade, until tender.

Grilled Market Veggies

Lisa Ann Panzino-DiNunzio, *Vineland, NJ*

Grilled Peaches

A unique way to serve up one of summer's sweet natural delights.

Serves 8

4 peaches, halved and pitted
2 T. butter, melted
cinnamon to taste
8 scoops vanilla ice cream or frozen yogurt

Brush the cut side of each peach half lightly with butter. Place peaches cut-side down on a hot grill. Reduce heat and grill for 8 to 10 minutes, until tender. Remove to serving bowls. Sprinkle with cinnamon. Top with a scoop of ice cream or frozen yogurt.

> ⎯ **New Flavor** ⎯
>
> **Many fruits as well as veggies grill very nicely.
> Try pears, apples and even Romaine lettuce.**

Diana Chaney, *Olathe, KS*

Corn Pudding

If you have it, try this dish using fresh sweet corn. Yum!

Serves 6 to 8

9 ears corn
4 eggs, beaten
$\frac{1}{2}$ c. half-and-half
$1\frac{1}{2}$ t. baking powder
$\frac{1}{3}$ c. butter
2 T. sugar
2 T. all-purpose flour
1 T. butter, melted
$\frac{1}{8}$ t. pepper

Remove and discard husks and silks from corn. Cut off tips of corn kernels into a bowl; scrape milk and remaining pulp from cob with a paring knife to measure 3 to 4 cups total. Set corn aside. Combine eggs, half-and-half and baking powder, stirring well with a wire whisk. Melt $\frac{1}{3}$ cup butter in a large saucepan over low heat; add sugar and flour, stirring until smooth. Remove from heat; gradually add egg mixture, whisking constantly until smooth. Stir in corn. Pour corn mixture into a greased one- or $1\frac{1}{2}$-quart casserole dish. Bake, uncovered, at 350 degrees for 40 to 45 minutes or until pudding is set. Drizzle with melted butter; sprinkle with pepper. Broil $5\frac{1}{2}$ inches from heat 2 minutes or until golden. Let stand 5 minutes before serving.

Corn Pudding

Mary Murray, *Mount Vernon, OH*

Fresh Salsa

Use those fresh summer ingredients to make this oh-so-yummy salsa to serve with grilled meats, veggies or favorite chips. Sitting by the pool just got even better!

Makes 3½ cups

1 jalapeño pepper, seeded and minced
1 cucumber, peeled and diced
4 plum tomatoes, chopped
½ c. fresh cilantro, finely chopped
2 T. vinegar
2 T. olive oil
1 t. sugar
1 t. ground cumin
½ t. salt
tortilla chips

Stir together all ingredients except tortilla chips in a small bowl. Cover and chill at least one hour. Serve with tortilla chips.

Sharon Demers, *Dolores, CO*

Firecracker Grilled Salmon

Add more red pepper flakes or a dusting of cayenne pepper for even more heat!

Serves 4

4 4- to 6-oz. salmon fillets
¼ c. peanut oil
2 T. soy sauce
2 T. balsamic vinegar
2 T. green onions, chopped
1½ t. brown sugar, packed
1 clove garlic, minced
½ t. red pepper flakes
½ t. sesame oil
⅛ t. salt

Place salmon in a glass baking pan. Whisk together remaining ingredients and pour over salmon. Cover with plastic wrap; refrigerate 4 to 6 hours. Remove salmon, discarding marinade. Place on an aluminum foil-lined grill that has been sprayed with non-stick vegetable spray. Grill 10 minutes per inch of thickness, measured at thickest part, until fish flakes easily with a fork. Turn halfway through cooking.

Firecracker Grilled Salmon

Sarah Kropf, *Richmond, VA*

New-Fangled Tuna Penne Casserole

The sour cream and wine gives this casserole a delicious tang.

Serves 2

2¼ c. whole-wheat penne pasta, uncooked
½ lb. sliced mushrooms
2 green onions, minced
¼ c. fresh Italian parsley, minced
1 to 2 6-oz. cans tuna, drained
8-oz. container sour cream
½ c. light mayonnaise
2 t. Dijon mustard
Optional: 2 T. dry white wine
½ c. shredded Cheddar cheese

Cook pasta according to package directions; drain and return to pan. Meanwhile, spray a skillet with non-stick vegetable spray. Add mushrooms, onions and parsley. Cook over medium heat until mushrooms are tender, about 5 minutes. Add tuna; cook until heated through. Stir tuna mixture into pasta; blend in sour cream, mayonnaise, mustard and wine, if using. Spread in a lightly greased 2-quart casserole dish. Top with cheese. Bake, uncovered, at 375 degrees for 30 minutes.

Amy Butcher, *Columbus, GA*

Garlicky Baked Shrimp

Here's the perfect party recipe...guests peel their own shrimp and save you the work!

Serves 6

2 lbs. uncooked large shrimp, rinsed and
    unpeeled
16-oz. bottle Italian salad dressing
1½ T. pepper
2 cloves garlic, pressed
2 lemons, halved
¼ c. fresh parsley, chopped
½ c. butter, cut into pieces

Place first 4 ingredients in a 13"x9" baking pan, tossing to coat. Squeeze juice from lemons over shrimp mixture and stir. Add lemon halves to pan. Sprinkle shrimp with parsley; dot with butter. Bake, uncovered, at 375 degrees for 25 minutes, stirring after 15 minutes. Serve in pan or in serving dish.

> ⚞ **Make it Easier** ⚟
> To bake this when you're on vacation, purchase a large disposable roasting pan for easy clean-up.

Garlicky Baked Shrimp

Nancie Flynn, *Bear Creek Township, PA*

Gram's Zucchini in a Pan

Gram used to serve this as a main dish in late summer when zucchini was plentiful.

Makes 6 servings

2 T. olive oil
1 onion, thinly sliced and separated into rings
4 to 5 sweet Italian peppers, sliced
2 zucchini, thinly sliced
2 tomatoes, diced
1 t. Italian seasoning
salt and pepper to taste
¾ c. shredded Cheddar cheese

Heat olive oil in a skillet over medium heat. Add onion and peppers; cover and cook until soft, about 5 minutes. Stir in zucchini, tomatoes and seasonings. Cover and cook to desired tenderness. Remove from heat; stir in cheese. Cover and let stand until cheese melts; serve warm.

Judy Bailey, *Des Moines, IA*

Grilled Chicken with White BBQ Sauce

Aromatic herbs scent the air when you grill this chicken seasoned with a dry rub. The flavors go well with a creamy white barbecue sauce spiced with tangy brown mustard and a spoonful of horseradish.

Serves 5

3 lbs. chicken thighs and drumsticks
1 T. dried thyme
1 T. dried oregano
1 T. ground cumin
1 T. paprika
1 t. onion powder
½ t. salt
½ t. pepper

Pat chicken dry with paper towels. Combine remaining ingredients; rub mixture evenly over chicken. Place chicken in a large plastic zipping bag. Seal and chill 4 hours. Remove chicken from bag, discarding bag. Grill, covered with grill lid, over medium-high heat (350 to 400 degrees) for 8 to 10 minutes on each side or until a meat thermometer inserted into thickest portion registers 165 degrees or to desired doneness. Serve with White BBQ Sauce.

WHITE BBQ SAUCE:
1½ c. mayonnaise
¼ c. white wine vinegar
1 clove garlic, minced
1 T. coarsely ground pepper
1 T. spicy brown mustard
1 t. sugar
1 t. salt
2 t. horseradish

Stir together all ingredients until well blended. Store in an airtight container in refrigerator at least 2 hours and up to one week. Makes 1¾ cups.

Grilled Chicken with White BBQ Sauce

Kelly Patrick, *Ashburn, VA*

Summer Squash Pie

My mother and I have used this recipe every summer when summer squash is abundant. Everyone always loves it and asks for the recipe!

Makes 6 to 8 servings

3 c. yellow squash, peeled and diced
½ c. onion, chopped
4 eggs, beaten
⅓ c. canola oil
1 c. biscuit baking mix
½ c. shredded part-skim mozzarella cheese
¼ t. pepper

Mix all ingredients in a bowl. Pat into a 9" pie plate lightly coated with non-stick vegetable spray. Bake at 350 degrees for 50 minutes to one hour, until set. Let stand for 10 minutes; slice into wedges. Serve warm or cold.

Jo Ann, *Gooseberry Patch*

Lettuce Wedge Salad

Who can resist a simple iceberg wedge, especially when it's icy cold?

Serves 4

4 to 6 slices bacon
1 onion, sliced
1 c. buttermilk
½ c. sour cream
1-oz. pkg. ranch salad dressing mix
¼ c. fresh basil, chopped
2 cloves garlic
1 head iceberg lettuce, cut into 4 wedges
Optional: shredded fresh basil

Cook bacon in a large skillet over medium heat until crisp; remove bacon and drain on paper towels, reserving one tablespoon drippings in skillet. Crumble bacon and set aside. Sauté onion in hot drippings in skillet over medium heat 10 minutes or until tender and lightly browned. Remove from heat; cool. Process onion, buttermilk and next 4 ingredients in a blender or food processor until smooth, stopping to scrape down sides. Top each lettuce wedge with dressing; sprinkle with bacon and top with shredded basil, if desired.

Note: You can make the dressing ahead and store it in the refrigerator. The chilled dressing will have a thicker consistency.

Lettuce Wedge Salad

Angie Cornelius, *Sheridan, IL*

Summer in a Bowl

We have a large, wonderful vegetable garden every summer. This salad makes excellent use of all those peppers, cucumbers and tomatoes.

Makes 4 servings

4 roma tomatoes, seeded and chopped
1 cubanelle pepper, seeded and chopped
1 cucumber, chopped
¼ c. red onion, minced
6 fresh basil leaves, shredded
salt and pepper to taste
4 c. Italian bread, sliced, cubed and toasted
3 T. olive oil

Combine vegetables, basil, salt and pepper in a bowl. Let stand at room temperature for 30 minutes. At serving time, stir in bread cubes; drizzle with oil. Mix thoroughly; serve at room temperature.

Edie DeSpain, *Logan, VT*

Spicy Cabbage-Apple Slaw

We love to serve this cool salad on hot summer nights with a grilled burger or steak. It is always a hit!

Makes 8 servings

2 c. shredded green and red cabbage mix
2 c. apples, cored and chopped
½ c. celery, chopped
2 T. walnuts, chopped and toasted
2 T. golden raisins
½ c. plain yogurt
2 T. apple juice
1 T. honey
½ t. cinnamon

In a large serving bowl, combine cabbage mix, apples, celery, nuts and raisins; toss well. Combine remaining ingredients in a small bowl, stirring well. Pour yogurt mixture over cabbage mixture; toss well. Cover and chill for at least 30 minutes before serving.

Spicy Cabbage-Apple Slaw

Jolene Koval, *Ontario, Canada*

Jolene's Chickpea Medley

This unusual salad goes together in jiffy! It's terrific for warm-weather meals grilled in the backyard.

Makes 6 servings

15-oz. can low-sodium garbanzo beans, drained and rinsed
1 red pepper, diced
1 c. kale, finely shredded
1 zucchini, chopped
1 ear fresh corn, kernels cut off, or ½ c. frozen corn, thawed
¼ c. Italian salad dressing

In a salad bowl, combine beans and vegetables. Drizzle with salad dressing; toss to mix. Let stand 15 minutes before serving to allow flavors to blend.

Cris Goode, *Mooresville, IN*

Good & Healthy "Fried" Chicken

We love this healthier version of everyone's favorite food...fried chicken!

Makes 5 servings

1 c. whole-grain panko bread crumbs
1 c. cornmeal
2 T. all-purpose flour
salt and pepper to taste
1 c. buttermilk
10 chicken drumsticks

Combine panko, cornmeal, flour, salt and pepper in a gallon-size plastic zipping bag. Coat chicken with buttermilk, one piece at a time. Drop chicken into bag and shake to coat pieces lightly. Arrange chicken on a baking pan coated with non-stick vegetable spray. Bake, uncovered, at 350 degrees for 40 to 50 minutes, until chicken juices run clear.

> ⌒ **Summer Picnic Idea** ⌒
> This chicken is yummy cold as well as hot. Pack a picnic lunch with the chicken, potato salad and a jug of lemonade...enjoy!

Good & Healthy "Fried" Chicken

Laurie Lightfoot, *Hawthorne, NV*

Fourth of July Beans

It's just not summer without this favorite side dish!

Serves 10 to 12

1 lb. bacon, diced
1 lb. ground beef
1 lb. hot ground pork sausage
1 c. onion, chopped
28-oz. can pork & beans
15-oz. can ranch-style beans
15-oz. can maple-flavored baked beans
16-oz. can kidney beans, drained and rinsed
½ c. barbecue sauce
½ c. catsup
½ c. brown sugar, packed
1 T. mustard
2 T. molasses
1 t. salt
½ t. chili powder

In a large Dutch oven over medium-high heat, cook bacon until crisp; drain, remove and set aside. Cook beef, sausage and onion until meat is browned; drain. Transfer to a greased disposable aluminum roasting pan. Stir in bacon and remaining ingredients; mix well. Cover and bake at 350 degrees for 45 minutes. Uncover and bake for 15 more minutes.

Stefanie Schmidt, *Las Vegas, NV*

Very Veggie Mac & Cheese

My mom used to sneak our vegetables into this dish. I loved the taste, and she loved that it was healthy and delicious. This is still my favorite comfort food dish because it tastes so good and reminds me of Mom.

Makes 8 servings

8-oz. pkg. whole-wheat elbow macaroni, uncooked
1 c. carrots, peeled and sliced
1 c. broccoli, chopped
1 c. cauliflower, chopped
1¼ c. milk
2 T. cornstarch
2 T. extra-virgin olive oil
1 red onion, chopped
4 cloves garlic, minced
½ c. shredded Monterey Jack cheese
½ c. shredded Cheddar cheese
¼ c. cream cheese

Prepare macaroni according to package directions; add vegetables to cooking water during the last 5 minutes of cooking time. Drain; place in a serving bowl. Meanwhile, whisk together milk and cornstarch in a bowl; set aside. Heat oil in a large saucepan over medium heat. Add onion and garlic; cook, stirring frequently, for about 5 minutes. Add milk mixture to onion mixture; bring to a boil, stirring constantly. Reduce heat to low; add cheeses. Cook and stir until cheeses are melted; pour over macaroni mixture. Toss until well combined.

Very Veggie Mac & Cheese

Nancy Molldrem, *Eau Claire, WI*

Grilled Parmesan Bread

We love to make this bread when we grill steaks or salmon. Add a salad and you have the perfect summer meal.

Serves 6

¼ c. butter, softened
½ c. grated Parmesan cheese
6 slices French bread, 1 inch thick

Blend butter and cheese in a small bowl. Spread mixture on both sides of bread slices. Place on a grill over medium heat. Toast until golden, about 3 minutes on each side.

⌐ Good Idea ⌐

To make the bread into an appetizer, remove from grill and add a spoonful of chopped tomato and cilantro. Delicious!

Rogene Rogers, *Bemidji, MN*

Raspberry & Chicken Salad

This salad make such a pretty lunch or dinner in the summertime. It is light, colorful and full of flavor!

Serves 6

1 c. low-sodium chicken broth
1 c. water
4 boneless, skinless chicken breasts
⅓ c. olive oil
3 T. raspberry vinegar
½ t. Dijon mustard
salt and pepper to taste
10-oz. pkg. mixed salad greens
1 pt. raspberries

Combine chicken broth and water in a saucepan over medium heat. Cover; bring to a boil. Reduce heat and add chicken. Cover and simmer 10 minutes, or until cooked through; drain. Let chicken cool and cut into ¼-inch slices. Combine olive oil, vinegar, mustard, salt and pepper in a small screw-top jar; shake well. In a large bowl, toss salad greens with ⅓ of dressing. In a blender, blend ⅓ cup of raspberries and remaining dressing until smooth. Arrange salad on individual serving plates; top with chicken and remaining raspberries. Drizzle with dressing; serve immediately.

Raspberry & Chicken Salad

Kelly Gray, *Weston, WV*

Spicy Carrot French Fries

Give potatoes the night off...kids will love these fries!

Makes 4 to 6 servings

2 lbs. carrots, peeled and cut into matchsticks
4 T. olive oil, divided
1 T. seasoned salt
2 t. ground cumin
1 t. chili powder
1 t. pepper
Garnish: ranch salad dressing

Place carrots in a plastic zipping bag. Sprinkle with 3 tablespoons oil and seasonings; toss to coat. Drizzle remaining oil in a shallow 13"x9" baking pan; arrange carrots in a single layer in pan. Bake, uncovered, at 425 degrees for 25 to 35 minutes, until carrots are golden. Serve with salad dressing for dipping.

Audrey Lett, *Newark, DE*

Marinated Sugar Snap Peas

This is an easy veggie dish that is perfect for summer celebrations. If you prepare this dish ahead of time, be sure to allow it to come to room temperature before serving.

Makes 8 servings

1½ lbs. sugar snap peas
½ red onion, thinly sliced
1 clove garlic, minced
¼ c. olive oil

Place peas in a large stockpot and add water to cover; bring to a boil and cook one minute, or until crisp-tender. Drain and rinse; place peas in a large bowl. Add onion, garlic and olive oil; toss gently. Cover and refrigerate at least 20 minutes. Remove from refrigerator and let stand. Serve at room temperature.

Marinated Sugar Snap Peas

Bob Gurlinger, *Kearney, NE*

Strawberry-Banana Smoothies

We try different fruit combinations all the time. Strawberry-banana is still my favorite.

Makes 2 servings

2 c. frozen strawberries
2 bananas, sliced and frozen
1 c. almond milk
2 T. creamy peanut butter
1 c. fresh spinach leaves
Garnish: shredded coconut, pecans,
    blueberries, strawberries, granola

In a blender, combine all ingredients except garnish; process well until smooth. Divide between 2 tall glasses; garnish as desired.

Francie Stutzman, *Dayton, OH*

That Yummy Bread

Homemade bread with a savory herb filling... really unforgettable!

Makes 2 loaves, serves 20

1 c. skim milk
2 T. sugar
¼ c. butter
2½ t. salt
1 c. water
2 envs. active dry yeast
7 c. all-purpose flour, divided
2 eggs, beaten and divided
1 T. butter, melted

In a medium saucepan, heat milk just to boiling; stir in sugar, butter and salt. Cool to lukewarm and set aside. Heat water until warm (110 to 115 degrees); add yeast, stir to dissolve and add to milk mixture. Pour into a large bowl and add 4 cups flour; stir and beat. Gradually add remaining flour; stir. Let dough rest 10 minutes; turn dough out onto a floured surface and knead until smooth. Place dough in a greased bowl, turning to coat. Cover and let rise in a warm place (85 degrees), away from drafts, until doubled in bulk. Punch down dough; shape into 2 balls. Roll out each ball into a ¼-inch-thick 15"x9" rectangle. Brush with 2 tablespoons egg, reserving remainder for filling. Spread Herb Filling to one inch from edges of dough; roll up jelly-roll style, starting at short edge. Pinch edges to seal; place in 2 greased 9"x5" loaf pans, seam-side down. Brush with butter; cover and let rise in a warm place 55 minutes. Slash tops of loaves with a knife; bake at 375 degrees for one hour. Let cool before slicing.

HERB FILLING:

2 c. fresh parsley, chopped
2 c. green onions, chopped
1 clove garlic, minced
2 T. butter
¾ t. salt
pepper and hot pepper
sauce to taste

Sauté parsley, onions and garlic in butter; cool slightly and add reserved egg from main recipe. Add salt, pepper and hot pepper sauce.

That Yummy Bread

Larry Anderson, *New Orleans, LA*

Herbed Zucchini & Bowties

A beautiful dish for a quick summer supper, plus you can use that wonderful zucchini in your garden!

Serves 4

2 T. butter
¼ c. oil, divided
1 onion, chopped
1 clove garlic, chopped
1 green pepper, diced
3 zucchini, halved lengthwise and sliced
1 t. dried parsley
1 t. dried rosemary, crumbled
1 t. dried basil
16-oz. pkg. bowtie pasta, cooked
½ c. shaved Parmesan cheese

In a skillet over medium heat, melt butter with 2 tablespoons oil. Add onion and garlic; sauté for 5 minutes. Stir in green pepper; sauté for an additional 3 minutes. Stir in zucchini and herbs; cover and cook over low heat for 5 to 8 minutes, until zucchini is tender. Add remaining oil; toss with bowties. Sprinkle with Parmesan cheese.

Beverly Mock, *Pensacola, FL*

Turkey Fruit Salad

Host a summertime luncheon with girlfriends and serve this delicious salad.

Serves 4

3 c. cooked turkey, cubed
¾ c. celery, chopped
1 c. seedless red grapes, halved
⅓ c. fresh pineapple, cubed
11-oz. can mandarin oranges, drained
¼ c. chopped pecans
¼ c. light mayonnaise-type salad dressing
⅛ t. salt
Garnish: lettuce leaves

Combine turkey, celery, grapes, pineapple, oranges and pecans together. Blend in salad dressing; sprinkle with salt. Chill until serving time. When ready to serve, spoon individual servings onto lettuce leaves.

Turkey Fruit Salad

Tiffany Brinkley, *Broomfield, CO*

Town Square Favorite

A visit with friends for the weekend took us to a farmers' market on the town square. We filled our baskets with veggies, herbs, even cheese! That same day, we made these yummy open-faced sandwiches for dinner.

Serves 4

3 T. butter
1½ c. sliced mushrooms
½ c. red onion, sliced and separated into rings
2 zucchini, thinly sliced
1 t. dried basil
½ t. garlic, finely chopped
¼ t. salt
¼ t. pepper
4 whole-wheat bagel thins, split
1 c. shredded Monterey Jack cheese, divided
2 tomatoes, sliced

Melt butter in a skillet over medium heat. Stir in all ingredients except bagels, cheese and tomatoes. Cook, stirring occasionally, until vegetables are crisp-tender, about 4 to 5 minutes. Arrange bagels on an ungreased baking sheet. Sprinkle one tablespoon cheese over each bagel half. Bake at 375 degrees for 5 minutes, or until cheese is melted. Remove from oven; top each with one slice tomato. Spoon on vegetable mixture; top with remaining cheese. Continue baking 4 to 5 minutes longer, until cheese is melted. Serve open-faced.

Sandra Sullivan, *Aurora, CO*

Beef & Snap Pea Stir-Fry

In a rush? Spice up tonight's dinner with my go-to recipe for healthy in a hurry! Substitute chicken or pork for the beef, if you like.

Makes 4 servings

1 c. brown rice, uncooked
1 lb. beef sirloin steak, thinly sliced
1 T. cornstarch
¼ t. salt
¼ t. pepper
2 t. canola oil
¾ c. water
1 lb. sugar snap peas, trimmed and halved
1 red pepper, cut into bite-size pieces
6 green onions, thinly sliced diagonally, white and green parts divided
1 T. fresh ginger, peeled and grated
½ t. red pepper flakes
salt and pepper to taste
2 T. lime juice

Cook rice according to package directions. Fluff with a fork; cover and set aside. Meanwhile, sprinkle beef with cornstarch, salt and pepper; toss to coat. Heat oil in a skillet over medium-high heat. Add half of beef and brown on both sides. Transfer to a plate; repeat with remaining beef. Stir in water, peas, red pepper, white part of onions, ginger and red pepper flakes; season with salt and pepper. Cook until peas turn bright green, one to 2 minutes. Return beef to skillet; cook for another 2 to 3 minutes. Remove from heat. Stir in lime juice and green part of onions. Serve over cooked rice.

Beef & Snap Pea Stir-Fry

Belva Conner, *Hillsdale, IN*

Tangy Watermelon Salad

Watermelon is one of the best things about summer and this recipe won't disappoint!

Makes about 10 servings

14 c. watermelon, cubed
1 red onion, halved and thinly sliced
1 c. green onions, chopped
¾ c. orange juice
5 T. red wine vinegar
2 T. plus 1½ t. honey
1 T. green pepper, finely chopped
½ t. salt
¼ t. pepper
¼ t. garlic powder
¼ t. onion powder
¼ t. dry mustard
¾ c. oil

In a large bowl, combine watermelon and onion; set aside. In a small bowl, combine orange juice, vinegar, honey, green pepper and seasonings; slowly whisk in oil. Pour over watermelon mixture; toss gently. Cover and refrigerate for at least 2 hours. Serve with a slotted spoon.

Jo Ann, *Gooseberry Patch*

Mexican Black Bean Burrito Bowls

This budget-friendly recipe is easy to double for a crowd at your summer picnic.

Makes 4 servings

2 c. brown rice, uncooked
15½-oz. can black beans, drained and rinsed
¼ c. water
½ t. chili powder
¼ t. ground cumin
½ t. salt, divided
1 T. olive oil
1 c. corn
1 T. fresh lime juice, divided
¼ c. fresh cilantro, chopped and divided
4 c. romaine lettuce, finely chopped
1 c. crumbled queso blanco or feta cheese
2 avocados, peeled, pitted and sliced
½ c. favorite salsa
¼ c. sour cream

Cook rice according to package directions; set aside. Meanwhile, in a saucepan over medium heat, combine beans, water, spices and ¼ teaspoon salt; cook until heated through. Cover and remove from heat. Heat oil in a skillet over medium-high heat; add corn and cook for about 5 minutes. Sprinkle with remaining salt and one teaspoon lime juice; set aside. Transfer cooked rice to a bowl; stir in 2 tablespoons cilantro and remaining lime juice. To serve, divide beans, corn, rice, lettuce, cheese and avocado among 4 bowls. Top with salsa, sour cream and remaining cilantro.

Mexican Black Bean Burrito Bowls

Lynda McCormick, *Burkburnett, TX*

Lynda's Salmon Burgers

My entire family loves these salmon burgers. I usually serve them with just-picked berries or fresh pineapple.

Makes 8 servings

1 lb. salmon fillet, skin removed and chopped
½ c. red onion, finely chopped
¼ c. fresh basil, thinly sliced
¼ t. salt
¼ t. pepper
1 egg white
1 T. sriracha hot chili sauce
Optional: ¼ c. panko bread crumbs
8 slices whole-grain bread, toasted and cut
   in half
Garnish: lettuce leaves, tomato slices

In a large bowl, combine salmon, onion, basil and seasonings; mix gently. In a small bowl, whisk together egg white and chili sauce. Add to salmon mixture and stir well to combine. If mixture is too soft, stir in bread crumbs if desired. Form mixture into 8 patties. Heat a large non-stick skillet over medium-high heat. Coat pan with non-stick vegetable spray. Add patties to skillet; cook for about 2 to 3 minutes per side. Place patties sandwich-style on toasted wheat bread. Garnish as desired.

Tabetha Moore, *New Braunfels, TX*

Super-Easy Stuffed Peppers

My husband says these are the best peppers!

Serves 4

4 green, red or orange peppers, tops removed
1 lb. ground beef
1 onion, diced
1 T. Italian seasoning
1 clove garlic, pressed
3 c. cooked brown rice
26-oz. can spaghetti sauce, divided
salt and pepper to taste
Garnish: shredded Parmesan cheese

Bring a large saucepan of water to a boil; add peppers and boil until tender. Drain and set aside. Brown ground beef with onion in a skillet; drain. Add Italian seasoning and garlic. Set aside ½ cup spaghetti sauce. Combine ground beef mixture, remaining sauce, cooked rice, salt and pepper in a bowl. Arrange peppers in a lightly greased 8"x8" baking pan. Fill peppers completely with ground beef mixture, spooning any extra mixture between peppers. Top with reserved sauce. Add pepper tops if using. Lightly cover with aluminum foil; bake at 400 degrees for 20 to 25 minutes. Sprinkle with Parmesan cheese.

Super-Easy Stuffed Peppers

Charlotte Harding, *Starkville, MS*

Summertime Iced Tea

Freeze sprigs of fresh mint in ice cubes for a party-pretty touch.

Makes 8 to 10 servings

4 c. boiling water
2 family-size tea bags
6 leaves fresh mint
6-oz. can frozen lemonade concentrate
1 c. sugar
5 c. cold water
Garnish: ice cubes, fresh mint sprigs

Pour boiling water into a large heatproof pitcher. Add tea bags and mint leaves; let stand for 5 minutes. Discard tea bags and mint leaves. Add frozen lemonade, sugar and cold water; mix well. Serve over ice, garnished with mint.

Carla Pfall, *Philadelphia, PA*

Grilled Chicken Tzatziki Bowls

I've made this with grilled steak and pork as well, whatever I happen to have on hand.

Makes 4 servings

¼ c. plain Greek yogurt
2 T. olive oil, divided
1 T. plus 1½ t. red wine vinegar, divided
2 cloves garlic, minced
½ t. dried oregano
1 lb. boneless, skinless chicken breasts, cut into one-inch cubes
¾ t. salt
¼ t. pepper
3 cucumbers, thinly sliced
1 c. cherry tomatoes, halved
¼ red onion, thinly sliced
2 c. cooked quinoa, warmed
1 c. tzatziki sauce
Garnish: sliced black olives, crumbled feta cheese

In a large bowl, whisk together yogurt, one tablespoon oil, 1½ teaspoons vinegar, garlic and oregano. Add chicken; stir to coat. Cover and refrigerate for one hour. Drain chicken, discarding marinade. Thread chicken pieces onto 4 skewers. Season with salt and pepper. Grill chicken over medium-high heat, turning skewers occasionally, until golden and cooked through; set aside. In a separate bowl, whisk together remaining oil and vinegar. Add cucumbers, tomatoes and onion; toss to combine. To serve, divide quinoa among 4 bowls. Top with cucumber mixture and tzatziki sauce. Garnish as desired; top each bowl with one chicken skewer.

> ⌁ **Store It** ⌁
>
> Fresh tzatziki sauce is easy to make! In a medium bowl, whisk together 1 cup plain Greek yogurt; 1 cucumber, seeded, finely grated and drained; 2 cloves minced garlic; 1 teaspoon lemon zest; 1 tablespoon fresh lemon juice and 2 tablespoons chopped, fresh dill. Season with salt and pepper. Chill until ready to serve.

Grilled Chicken Tzatziki Bowls

Marilyn Morel, *Keene, NH*

Marilyn's Spaghetti Salad

A great dish for gatherings and picnics...easy to make and packed with veggies.

Serves 8

16-oz. pkg. spaghetti, uncooked
2 cucumbers, peeled, seeded and diced
2 tomatoes, diced
3 green onions, chopped
½ green pepper, chopped
½ red pepper, chopped
8-oz. bottle sun-dried tomato vinaigrette
    salad dressing
salt and pepper to taste

Cook spaghetti according to package directions; drain and rinse with cold water. In a 13"x9" glass baking pan, combine spaghetti and vegetables. Add salad dressing; toss gently to coat well. Cover and refrigerate several hours to overnight. Season with salt and pepper at serving time.

Nancy Wise, *Little Rock, AR*

Homestyle Green Beans

We have a garden and love to grow our own vegetables. This combination of green beans and grape tomatoes makes good use of two of our favorite home-grown veggies!

Serves 8

2 lbs. fresh green beans, trimmed
2 c. water
1¼ t. salt, divided
⅓ c. butter or margarine
1½ T. sugar
1 t. dried basil
½ t. garlic powder
¼ t. pepper
2 c. cherry or grape tomatoes, halved

Place beans in a Dutch oven; add water and one teaspoon salt. Bring to a boil; cover, reduce heat and simmer 15 minutes or until tender. Drain; keep warm. Melt butter in a saucepan over medium heat; stir in sugar, basil, garlic powder, remaining ¼ teaspoon salt and pepper. Add tomatoes and cook, stirring gently until thoroughly heated. Pour tomato mixture over beans and toss gently. Serve hot.

Homestyle Green Beans

Evelyn Moriarty, *Philadelphia, PA*

Vegetable Quinoa Patties

This recipe is my own, adapted from one I found online and tweaked. It has become a family favorite, especially in summertime when fresh-picked veggies are available.

Makes 6 servings

3 eggs
½ c. shredded part-skim mozzarella cheese
½ c. cottage cheese
¼ c. whole-wheat flour
1 carrot, peeled and grated
1 zucchini, grated
3 T. green, red or yellow pepper, grated
3 green onions, finely chopped
½ t. ground cumin
¼ t. garlic powder
⅛ t. salt
¼ t. pepper
2 c. cooked quinoa
1 T. olive oil

Beat eggs in a large bowl; stir in cheeses and flour, blending well. Mix in vegetables. Combine seasonings; sprinkle over vegetable mixture and mix well. Add cooked quinoa; stir together well. Heat olive oil in a skillet over medium heat. With a small ladle, drop mixture into skillet, making 6 patties. Flatten lightly with ladle to about ¼-inch thick. Fry patties for 4 to 5 minutes per side, until golden. Serve each serving with 3 tablespoons Dilled Yogurt Dressing.

DILLED YOGURT DRESSING:
½ c. plain Greek yogurt
1 cucumber, peeled and diced
3 sprigs fresh dill, snipped, or ½ t. dill weed

Stir together all ingredients in a small bowl.

Jill Ball, *Highland, UT*

Sweet & Tangy Fruit Dip

As a mother, I'm always looking for easy, healthy snack ideas, so I created this recipe.

Makes 10 servings

1 c. low-fat cottage cheese
3 T. low-fat plain yogurt
2 t. honey
1 T. orange juice
2½ T. orange marmalade
2 T. unsweetened flaked coconut
favorite fresh fruit, sliced

Place all ingredients except coconut and fruit in a food processor. Process until smooth and creamy. Stir in coconut. Refrigerate until chilled. Serve with a variety of fresh fruit.

Sweet & Tangy Fruit Dip

Patsy Sye, *Statesboro, GA*

Million-Dollar Pound Cake

We love to serve this cake with fresh sliced peaches or strawberries for a summer dessert.

Serves 10 to 12

2 c. butter, softened
3 c. sugar
6 eggs
4 c. all-purpose flour
¾ c. milk
1 t. almond extract
1 t. vanilla extract
Optional: sweetened whipped cream,
    blueberries, sliced peaches

Beat butter at medium speed with an electric mixer until light yellow in color and creamy. Gradually add sugar, beating at medium speed until light and fluffy. Add eggs, one at a time, beating just until yellow disappears after each addition. Add flour to butter mixture alternately with milk, beginning and ending with flour. Beat at low speed just until blended after each addition. (Batter should be smooth.) Stir in extracts. Pour batter into a greased and floured 10" tube pan. Bake at 300 degrees for one hour and 40 minutes or until a long wooden pick inserted in center comes out clean. Cool in pan on a wire rack 10 to 15 minutes. Remove from pan and cool completely on wire rack. Garnish each serving with whipped cream, blueberries and sliced peaches, if desired.

Carol Field Dahlstrom, *Ankeny, IA*

S'More Pops

Bring summertime fun inside when you make these toasted marshmallow s'more pops.

Makes 9

9 graham crackers
2 chocolate candy bars
9 marshmallows
9 pretzel sticks

Lay the graham crackers on a baking sheet. Place 2 squares of chocolate candy bar on each cracker. Use a knife to make a small slit in the bottom of each marshmallow. Push the pretzel rod into the marshmallow. Lay the marshmallow and stick on top of the chocolate bar. Heat oven to low broil. Watching carefully while heating, put the pan in the oven and heat until the marshmallows are just golden and chocolate melts. (This will take only a minute or less.) Remove from oven. Push pretzel further into the warm marshmallow. Let cool before picking up.

> ∼ **Vintage Finds** ∼
>
> Look for vintage pie tins, servers and cake plates at flea markets...add them to your collection or make them part of the gift when sharing a favorite sweet treat.

S'More Pops

Marlene Darnell, *Newport Beach, CA*

Fourth of July Lemon Bars

With a few simple decorations, your dessert will be the hit of the picnic!

Makes 6

16½-oz. pkg. lemon bar mix
¼ c. powdered sugar
.68-oz. tube red decorating gel
¼ c. blueberries

Prepare lemon bars as directed on package; bake in an ungreased 9"x9" baking pan. Cool completely in pan on a wire rack. Cut into 6 rectangular bars. Place bars on a serving plate. Sprinkle with powdered sugar. Pipe stripes across bars with decorating gel. Place 6 blueberries in the top corner of each bar.

Sharon Tillman, *Hampton, VA*

Pineapple Upside-Down Cupcakes

This classic recipe is a perfect dessert for a Father's Day celebration.

Makes 12 cupcakes

20-oz. can pineapple tidbits, drained and
  ½ c. juice reserved
⅓ c. brown sugar, packed
⅓ c. butter, melted
1 c. all-purpose flour
¾ c. sugar
½ t. baking powder
¼ c. butter, softened
1 egg, beaten
Garnish: maraschino cherries

Pat pineapple dry with paper towels. In a bowl, combine brown sugar and melted butter; divide mixture evenly into 12 greased muffin cups. Arrange pineapple chunks over brown sugar mixture. In a bowl, combine flour, sugar and baking powder. Mix in softened butter and reserved pineapple juice; beat for 2 minutes. Beat in egg. Spoon batter over pineapple, filling each cup ¾ full. Bake at 350 degrees for 30 minutes, or until a toothpick tests clean. Cool in pan for 5 minutes. Place a wire rack on top of muffin tin and invert cupcakes onto rack so pineapple is on top. Cool completely and top each with a cherry.

Pineapple Upside-Down Cupcakes

Barbara Parham Hyde, *Manchester, TN*

Stuffed Strawberries

Try using pecans in place of the walnuts for added variety.

Makes 18

20 strawberries, hulled and divided
8-oz. pkg. cream cheese, softened
¼ c. walnuts, finely chopped
1 T. powdered sugar
Optional: fresh mint leaves

Dice 2 strawberries; set aside. Cut a thin layer from the stem end of the remaining strawberries, forming a base. Starting at opposite end of strawberry, slice into 4 wedges, being careful not to slice through the base; set aside. Beat remaining ingredients together until fluffy; fold in diced strawberries. Spoon 1½ tablespoonfuls into the center of each strawberry. Refrigerate until ready to serve. Garnish with fresh mint leaves, if desired.

Michelle Case, *Yardley, PA*

Breakfast Berry Parfait

So pretty served in simple wine glasses or champagne flutes!

Serves 2

1 c. bran & raisin cereal, divided
6-oz. container strawberry yogurt
1 c. strawberries, hulled
½ c. raspberries
¼ c. blackberries

Layer half the cereal and all of the yogurt in the 2 glasses. Add berries and top with more cereal.

Eleanor Bamford, *Boonton, NJ*

Summer Sparkle

Serve in tall fluted glasses with plenty of ice... oh-so refreshing!

Makes 16 to 20 servings

48-oz. bottle ruby red grapefruit juice
12-oz. can frozen orange juice concentrate, thawed
6-oz. can frozen lemonade concentrate, thawed
2-ltr. bottle lemon-lime soda, chilled
Optional: lemon slices, fresh mint sprigs

In a one-gallon pitcher, stir together all juices; cover and refrigerate until chilled. At serving time, add soda; garnish as desired. Serve immediately.

Summer Sparkle

Vickie, *Gooseberry Patch*

Watermelon Fruitsicles

Everyone loves watermelon! This is the perfect pool-party treat.

Makes one dozen

5-lb. watermelon wedge, seeded and cubed
½ c. sugar
1 env. unflavored gelatin
1 T. lemon juice

Place half of watermelon in container of an electric blender; process until smooth. Repeat procedure with remaining watermelon. Strain watermelon purée into a large measuring cup, discarding pulp. Reserve 4 cups watermelon juice. Combine one cup juice and sugar in a saucepan. Sprinkle gelatin over mixture; let stand one minute. Cook over medium heat, stirring constantly, until sugar and gelatin dissolve. Add gelatin mixture to remaining 3 cups watermelon juice; stir in lemon juice and let cool. Pour into ⅓-cup frozen pop molds; freeze.

Jennifer Peterson, *Ankeny, IA*

Patriotic Cupcakes

This cupcake arrangement makes an American flag for the perfect Fourth of July celebration or Memorial Day event.

Makes 2 dozen

2 c. sugar
1 c. butter, softened
2 eggs
2 t. lemon juice
1 t. vanilla extract
2½ c. cake flour
½ t. baking soda
1 c. buttermilk
Garnish: 16-oz. can white frosting; red, white and blue sprinkles

Beat sugar and butter at medium speed with an electric mixer until creamy. Add eggs, one at a time, beating until yellow disappears after each addition. Beat in lemon juice and vanilla. Combine flour and baking soda in a small bowl; add to sugar mixture alternately with buttermilk, beginning and ending with flour mixture. Beat at medium speed just until blended after each addition. Spoon batter into paper-lined muffin cups, filling ⅔ full. Bake at 350 degrees for 18 to 22 minutes or until a toothpick inserted in center comes out clean. Cool in pans on a wire rack 10 minutes. Remove cupcakes from pans to wire rack; cool 45 minutes or until completely cool. Spread frosting on cupcakes. Immediately decorate with desired red, white and blue sprinkles. Place cupcakes on plate in a flag pattern.

> ~ **Edible Centerpiece** ~
>
> A heaping plate of cookies, bars, cupcakes or cake squares makes a delightful (and delicious) centerpiece at a casual gathering with friends.

Patriotic Cupcakes

Lillian Dahlstrom, *Ames, IA*

Blueberry & Cheese Coffee Cake

This moist blueberry cream cheese cake with a lemon-sugar topping is special enough for company.

Serves 16

½ c. plus 2 T. butter, softened and divided
1¾ c. sugar, divided
2 eggs
2½ c. all-purpose flour, divided
1 t. baking powder
1 t. salt
¾ c. milk
¼ c. water
2 c. fresh blueberries
8-oz. pkg. cream cheese, cut into ¼-inch cubes
2 T. lemon zest

Beat ½ cup butter at medium speed with an electric mixer until creamy; gradually add 1¼ cups sugar, beating well. Add eggs, one at a time, beating until blended after each addition. Combine 2 cups flour, baking powder and salt; stir well. Combine milk and water; stir well. Add flour mixture to butter mixture alternately with milk mixture, beginning and ending with flour mixture. Mix at low speed after each addition until mixture is blended. Gently stir in blueberries and cream cheese. Pour batter into a greased 9"x9" baking pan. Combine lemon zest and remaining flour, sugar and butter; stir well with a fork. Sprinkle mixture over batter. Bake at 375 degrees for 55 minutes or until golden. Serve warm or let cool completely on a wire rack.

Jill Valentine, *Jackson, TN*

Homemade Vanilla Ice Cream

When I was young, we'd have what we called an "ice cream supper." We would pile in the car and head to the ice cream parlor...that really hit the spot on a hot summer night!

Serves 12

2½ c. whipping cream
2 c. half-and-half
2 eggs, beaten
1 c. sugar
¼ t. salt
2¼ t. vanilla extract
Optional: whole strawberries

Combine all ingredients except vanilla and optional strawberries in a heavy saucepan over medium-low heat, stirring constantly until mixture is thick enough to coat the back of a spoon and reaches 160 degrees on a candy thermometer. Remove from heat and stir in vanilla. Set pan in an ice-filled bowl; stir. Cover and chill in refrigerator for 8 hours or up to 24 hours. Pour mixture into ice cream maker and freeze according to manufacturer's directions. Garnish with whole strawberries, if desired.

> ⟞ **Did You Know?** ⟝
>
> The American tradition of serving coffee and sweet cake along with gossip actually evolved from the tradition of English tea.

Homemade Vanilla Ice Cream

Melissa Luck, *West Plains, MO*

Peach Flip-Overs

I had so many peaches from the farmers' market that I popped the extras in the freezer. Try them with peach ice cream...perfect for this recipe!

Makes 8 servings

2 to 3 peaches, pitted, peeled and sliced
2 t. butter
¼ t. nutmeg
1 t. cinnamon
2 to 3 T. pumpkin pie spice
1 t. brown sugar, packed
¼ c. sugar
1 to 2 t. vanilla extract
8-oz. tube refrigerated crescent rolls
ground ginger to taste
Garnish: powdered sugar, cinnamon

Add peaches, butter, spices, sugars and vanilla to a saucepan over medium heat. Simmer for 10 minutes; reduce heat to low. Separate and arrange crescent roll dough on a lightly greased baking sheet; sprinkle with ginger. Bake at 375 degrees for 5 minutes. Remove from oven and top each with one tablespoon peach mixture. Roll into a crescent; secure with a toothpick. Return to the oven for 5 to 10 minutes, or until golden. Sprinkle with powdered sugar.

Jill Ball, *Highland, UT*

Melon-Berry Bowls

I am always looking for quick, healthy and yummy breakfast ideas for my teenagers. This one has become a favorite!

Serves 2 to 4

1 honeydew melon, halved and seeded
6-oz. container favorite-flavor yogurt
½ c. blueberries
1 c. granola cereal

Use a melon baller to scoop honeydew into balls. Combine melon balls with remaining ingredients. Spoon into individual bowls to serve.

Zoe Bennet, *Columbia, SC*

Fruity Fresh Sorbet

So cool and refreshing for any summer get-together.

Makes 4 servings

1 peach, peeled, pitted and cubed
1 c. mango, peeled, pitted and cubed
1 ripe banana, peeled and mashed
4 T. water
1 T. lemon juice

Place fruit on a wax paper-lined baking sheet. Cover and freeze for about 2 hours, until completely frozen. Combine fruit, water and lemon juice in a food processor; process until smooth. Serve immediately, or spoon into a covered container and freeze up to 2 weeks.

Fruity Fresh Sorbet

Index

Desserts

Index

U. S. to Metric Recipe Equivalents

Volume Measurements

¼ teaspoon	1 mL
½ teaspoon	2 mL
1 teaspoon	5 mL
1 tablespoon = 3 teaspoons	15 mL
2 tablespoons = 1 fluid ounce	30 mL
¼ cup	60 mL
⅓ cup	75 mL
½ cup = 4 fluid ounces	125 mL
1 cup = 8 fluid ounces	250 mL
2 cups = 1 pint = 16 fluid ounces	500 mL
4 cups = 1 quart	1 L

Weights

1 ounce	30 g
4 ounces	120 g
8 ounces	225 g
16 ounces = 1 pound	450 g

Baking Pan Sizes

Square

8x8x2 inches	2 L = 20x20x5 cm
9x9x2 inches	2.5 L = 23x23x5 cm

Rectangular

13x9x2 inches	3.5 L = 33x23x5 cm

Loaf

9x5x3 inches	2 L = 23x13x7 cm

Round

8x1½ inches	1.2 L = 20x4 cm
9x1½ inches	1.5 L = 23x4 cm

Recipe Abbreviations

t. = teaspoon	ltr. = liter
T. = tablespoon	oz. = ounce
c. = cup	lb. = pound
pt. = pint	doz. = dozen
qt. = quart	pkg. = package
gal. = gallon	env. = envelope

Oven Temperatures

300° F	150° C
325° F	160° C
350° F	180° C
375° F	190° C
400° F	200° C
450° F	230° C

Kitchen Measurements

A pinch = ⅛ tablespoon
1 fluid ounce = 2 tablespoons
3 teaspoons = 1 tablespoon
4 fluid ounces = ½ cup
2 tablespoons = ⅛ cup
8 fluid ounces = 1 cup
4 tablespoons = ¼ cup
16 fluid ounces = 1 pint
8 tablespoons = ½ cup
32 fluid ounces = 1 quart
16 tablespoons = 1 cup
16 ounces net weight = 1 pound
2 cups = 1 pint
4 cups = 1 quart
4 quarts = 1 gallon